The INVADERS

The INVADERS

A Quinn Martin TV Series

JAMES ROSIN

Published by THE AUTUMN ROAD COMPANY, Philadelphia, PA

Design: Ronald Dorfman
www.RonaldDorfmanDesign.com

ISBN: 978-0972-868464

For…

LARRY COHEN,
an imaginative writer;

ROY THINNES,
a thoughtful actor
and devoted father;

and in memory of
QUINN MARTIN
the renowned executive
producer;
and
ALAN ARMER,
the gentleman producer.

CONTENTS

ACKNOWLEDGEMENTS

I EXPRESS MY GRATITUDE to the following people for taking time to contribute to this book: Howard Alston, Alan Armer, Carl Barth, Larry Cohen, Robert Day, Don Eitner, John Elizalde, William Hale, Tom Lowell, David Rintels, Ralph Senensky, Duane Tatro, Roy Thinnes, Paul Wurtzel, and Glenn Wilder.

Also special thanks to Ned Comstock of the USC Cinematic Arts Library, Joel Blumberg of Silver Screen Audio, and television historian Stephen Bowie for his insightful commentary taken from his in-depth essay on the series.

Highly recommend are the official DVD releases of the *The Invaders* by CBS/Paramount. Available are season one, season two, and both seasons combined. All have excellent picture quality, with nice packaging and arrangment of the DVDs.

THE INVADERS
About the Series

THE INVADERS debuted on Tuesday night, January 10, 1967 at 8:30 P.M. on the ABC Television Network.

The one-hour sci-fi series was created by Larry Cohen who began his career writing TV scripts for *Kraft Television Theater, Zane Grey Theater* and *U.S. Steel Hour.* In the early 1960s, Cohen scripted episodic television shows such as *Checkmate, Sam Benedict,* the pilot for *Arrest and Trial* (the precursor to *Law and Order), The Nurses,* as well as multiple stories and teleplays for *The Defenders,* the prestigious court-room drama that starred E. G. Marshall and Robert Reed. In 1964, Cohen created *Branded,* the western television series that starred Chuck Connors (who had co-starred with Ben Gazzara in the 90-minute *Arrest and Trial).*

At that point, the New York writer had a very receptive audience to his creative ideas.

LARRY COHEN
(Creator)

The inception of *The Invaders* began in 1966 when I met with Edgar Scherick and Douglas Cramer who were in charge of creative affairs at ABC. In those days, you could actually meet with the top network execu-tives who made the decisions with regard to buying and developing your project.

The concept that I presented was a science

fiction reality show done in the context of modern dress. It would be unlike the other network sci-fi series of that era set in the future, past, or situated on other planets with people wearing bubble helmets. My show was set in the major cities and towns of our country. It would be presented a little like Alfred Hitchcock's *39 Steps* or *Saboteur* where enemies existed within our country, and the lead character was the only one who knew of their existence.[1]

In Cohen's premise, a young Santa Barbara architect named David Vincent sees an alien spacecraft land and tries to convince "a disbelieving world." Cohen gave his lead character the last name of "Vincent" in honor of Vincent Price who had appeared in a number of horror films throughout the 1950s and early 1960s.

LARRY COHEN

The aliens that Vincent had to contend with came from another galaxy in the universe to take over our society. [Eventually it was established that they came from a dying planet.] The aliens appeared in human form and we never really knew their true appearance.

Some of them were emotionless, while some did have emotions. I felt they were more interesting if they had emotions instead of being cardboard characters for David Vincent to eliminate. What I felt was important was to create aliens who had defects that made them vulnerable. Even though they might have been a superior culture and intellect, they had to have a weakness. Something all powerful and undefeatable becomes uninteresting. The first thing I introduced was that they had to return to a regeneration chamber on a regular basis (every 10–12 days) or they would revert to their natural alien form.

I also took something from Hitchcock's *39 Steps* where the leader of an espionage ring was identifiable by a missing finger. I thought what if the aliens had a distorted pinky finger that would be a giveaway? In my script, the aliens were constantly trying to correct that to maintain their anonymity. The aliens had no heartbeat, no pulse, never bled, and when they perished, it was my idea to have them gradually incinerate, and show the agony in their demise. (When the series began it happened much more quickly.)[1]

Cohen's concept was suspenseful. Vincent not only hunted the aliens but was in turn hunted himself. As the stories unfolded, you wouldn't know who was and who wasn't an alien bent on the earth's destruction. Vincent, as a man in the know, could never be sure whether those from whom he sought help were those from whom he should flee.

In his meeting with the two network executives, Cohen presented *The Invaders* as a serial, to be broadcast in two half-hour episodes weekly, each ending in a cliffhanger.

LARRY COHEN

Batman was presented in the format I envisioned for *The Invaders* and *Peyton Place,* the first nighttime soap opera aired biweekly. In addition, there were numerous thirty-minute dramatic shows on the air at the time, and in those days it was economically feasible.[1]

Both Scherick and Cramer were receptive to Cohen's presentation, and they made a deal with him almost immediately. Cohen was commissioned to write a thirty-minute pilot, and provided about fifteen storylines as well.

At that point, the network brought in Quinn Martin, one of their top television producers. After producing the two-part episode of *The Untouchables* for *Desilu Playhouse,* and the subsequent first season of the series, Martin formed his own company—Q.M. Productions. His first TV series to air on ABC was *The New Breed* (1961–1962), a one-hour police drama that starred Leslie Nielsen. This was followed by *The Fugitive* (1963–1967) with David Janssen; *Twelve O'Clock High* with Robert Lansing (and later Paul Burke) (1964–1967), and *The F.B.I.* (1965–1974) which starred Efrem Zimbalist, Jr.

LARRY COHEN

When Quinn was brought in, I was getting a premier producer attached to the project and I was elated. I had worked with him previously on *The Fugitive* when I wrote the story for one episode and the teleplay for another entitled "Escape into Black." (That particular script redefined the original concept and was very well-received.) We got along very well and had a good working relationship.[1]

However, when Martin took control of the series, creative differences arose between him and Cohen.

LARRY COHEN

Quinn wanted to do *The Invaders* as a one-hour show that fit the formula he followed for his other series, beginning with a prologue, followed by Acts 1–4, and an epilogue. There was really no creative collaboration between us and Quinn hired another writer to rewrite my pilot.[1]

Cohen was paid handsomely for his creation and received a substantial profit from the series. Most of the storylines that he provided (when he created the project) were used in varying degrees during the first season. However, he no longer had any creative input into the show.

After creating another series for CBS *(Coronet Blue* starring Frank Converse), Cohen embarked on a prolific career as a writer/producer/director of his own feature films, occasionally doing TV projects such as *Never Too Young, Custer, Cool Million, Griff,* and *Columbo.*

A pilot for *The Invaders* was filmed in 1966 and the reaction from the television industry was very positive.

ALAN ARMER

(Series Producer 1967–1968)

When we finished putting all the pieces together, the pilot episode ("Beachhead") was 90 minutes, and it was marvelous. It was believable, involving, masterfully written by Anthony Wilson, and beautifully directed by Joseph Sargent. Good directors (like Joe) extract the most from every scene. They look for human values and in realizing the potential of that scene, it becomes longer. My agent told me it was the best pilot he had ever seen. Unfortunately, we had to edit it down to 60 minutes. Quinn implored the network to broadcast it in the longer format, but they couldn't do it due to commercial commitments.

When you're dealing with a premise as eventful and imaginative as ours was, part of what you try to do as a producer is make it believable.

You add those human elements I spoke of to accomplish that. In editing it down, you eliminate a lot of the interim material that contributes to that believability. What you're left with are the dramatic peaks. In our case, the result was okay, but what we had in the long-form version was very special.[2]

Cast in the lead role of David Vincent was Roy Thinnes. Originally from Chicago, Thinnes first appeared in an unsold pilot *(Chicago 212)* that starred Frank Lovejoy. During the early 1960s he appeared in network series such as *The Untouchables*, *Gunsmoke* and *The Eleventh Hour*. In 1963, he landed the role of Dr. Phil Brewer on *General Hospital*. Following a two-year stint on the daytime drama, Thinnes was cast as Ben Quick in *The Long Hot Summer* (an ABC series) opposite Edmund O'Brien and Nancy Malone. After its cancellation, Thinnes was signed to star in *The Invaders* and along the way guest starred in episodes of *The F.B.I.* and *The Fugitive*.

RALPH SENENSKY
(Director)

I directed Roy in *The Long Hot Summer* and in an episode of *The F.B.I.* prior to his starring role in *The Invaders*. I found him to be an intelligent and sensitive actor who did his homework, came to the set well prepared and the camera loved him.[3]

DON EITNER
(Actor: "Panic" *and* "Valley of the Shadow"*)*

I worked with Roy in two segments of *The Invaders* and I liked his approach to acting along with his work ethic. He was very responsive to his fellow actors. I felt there was a lot of truth and realism in his portrayal.[4]

MARSHALL SCHLOM
(Script Supervisor: Season One)

Roy was one of the few actors I worked with who believed in a sense of family on the set. There was no pretense about him. He treated everyone with respect and dignity.[5]

LARRY COHEN

Roy was a good choice for David Vincent. He was perfectly valid as a driven man out to convince the people he encountered of an alien invasion.[1]

ROY THINNES

When I first read the script for *The Invaders*, I was certainly interested because Quinn Martin, one of the most successful television producers that ever lived, was doing it. However, I was a bit skeptical about sci-fi, so Quinn invited me to a writer's conference. He said, "I don't want this to be a show with a lot of special effects, hardware and nonsense [which was faithful to the foundation that Larry Cohen had created]. I want this to be a study in paranoia. One man knowing a fact and not being able to convince anyone else" [a premise that already existed on *The Fugitive*].

That raised my curiosity and interest. He was looking for drama and it had to be in the material. It was a concept where you're trying to convince the world that it's in danger and that we're being infiltrated. That's good stuff to play and great food for an actor.[6]

DON EITNER

What was exciting about the role of David Vincent was that he had so many conflicts; and the more conflict you have the better the drama and the more involving it becomes.[4]

The character of David Vincent had much to contend with: an awareness of an alien presence, fear of their power and intentions, attempting to sell that seemingly incredulous idea to the people he encountered, not knowing who to trust and trying to save mankind in the process, were quite a set of conflicts to work through.

Thinnes' complex portrayal of David Vincent was edgy and intense in waging his silent war against an unseen enemy. Along the way he could be vindictive and merciless. In "Vikor" he sets up collaborator George Vikor to perish at the hands of the aliens. In "Summit Meeting, Part Two," he kills an alien in retribution for the death of his friend Mike Tressider. In "The Prophet" he shows no compassion for an emotionally distraught Sister Claire.

Yet there are many instances where his sensibilities are illuminated. In "The Leeches" Vincent displays genuine sorrow when told several people didn't survive his attempted rescue. In "Wall of Crystal" he offers his life in exchange for the life of his brother Robert (Linden Chiles), an alien hostage. In "Dark Outpost" he places his life in jeopardy to spare the lives of five students. Despite his desperation in "The Believers," his compassion is very apparent when Elyse Reynolds (Carol Lynley) talks of her brother's demise. In "The Innocent" we see an entirely different side of Vincent when he's transported to an idyllic setting and reunited with Helen (Katherine Justice), a woman he once loved. He displays a warmth and effervescence that's a nice departure from the series' usual serious tone.

More than the average amount of attention focused on *The Invaders* when it debuted on ABC as a mid-season replacement, partly because it was a Quinn Martin production, and because it was the first series with a premise of flying saucer occupants among us in human form.

The show's beginning was designed to attract viewer attention and orient them immediately. After the teaser and opening titles came a brief series of scenes which set up the show's premise. First, we see an alien spacecraft en route to earth from the point of view of two alien pilots in a second spacecraft. Narrator William Woodson in an ominous baritone voice explains that "alien beings from a dying planet are destined for earth to make it their world."

An abbreviated sequence (taken from the pilot) follows where David Vincent pulls off of a deserted country road in search of a diner and, in need of rest, falls asleep. In the early morning hours he's awakened by the landing of a flying saucer. Woodson continues, "Now David Vincent knows that the invaders are here, that they have taken human form. Somehow he must convince a disbelieving world that the nightmare has already begun."

The aliens appeared almost exclusively in human form. However, in two episodes we witness two different forms of reversion. In "Genesis" we see the vague outline of an amphibious creature submerged into an underwater tank at a sea lab installation for regeneration. In "The Enemy," Blake (Richard Anderson), the wounded alien survivor of a saucer crash, begins to revert as the story develops. First we notice his hands, then the metamorphosis of his head in the finale.

The aliens, basically portrayed as cold-blooded invaders out to destroy humanity, attempted to kill David Vincent on numerous occasions. Depending on the situation, the extraterrestrials would also try to take advantage of him to further their own ends. In "The Experiment," they subject him to brainwashing. In "The Innocent," the aliens attempt to convince Vincent of their aim to help humanity via an induced dream. In "Wall of Crystal," they kidnap his brother and resort to blackmail.

Not all of the aliens we meet are arch villains. In "Beachhead," Kathy Adams (Diane Baker) shows concern about Vincent's welfare and advises him not to resist them. In "The Mutation," Vikki (Suzanne Pleshette) develops feelings for Vincent and wants to stay with him. In "The Life Seekers," Keith (Barry Morse) and Claire (Diana Muldaur) are civilized and thoughtful aliens who disapprove of the planned invasion. They seek to return to their planet and persuade their leaders to abort their mission of conquest.

Ironically, Vincent sometimes finds himself allied with his adversaries. In "Valley of the Shadow," he hatches a plan with alien cooperation to prevent an entire town of people from being annihilated. In "Summit Meeting," he teams with alien Ellie

Markham (Diana Hyland) who disapproves of her compatriots' plans to assassinate world leaders. In "The Captive" he works feverishly to free an alien prisoner (Don Dubbins) to prevent a Russian embassy from being destroyed. In "The Peacemaker," he works in concert with the invaders to prevent a bomb from being dropped on a meeting of top alien leaders and U.S. military officials. In "The Life Seekers," he aids the two aforementioned fugitive aliens who choose to save mankind.

In his quest to convince "a disbelieving world," David Vincent travels a lonely path. Along the way he does succeed in enlightening others (ultimately he recruits a group of believers), but en route fate intervenes. In "The Experiment," Professor Curtis Lindstrom (Laurence Naismith) and his son Lloyd (Roddy McDowell) both perish at the hands of the aliens. In "The Leeches," several scientists rescued from the aliens are mentally impaired. In "Nightmare," Ellen Woods (Kathleen Widdoes) and Ed Gidney (James Callahan) are both afraid to reveal what they've seen. In "Genesis," when police lieutenant Greg Lucather (John Larch) offers to go to the F.B.I. and share his revelation, no evidence remains to support his claims of an alien occurrence.

Eyewitness accounts become meaningless because the aliens always destroy any evidence (including themselves) that supports their existence and there is always an explanation to account for what happened.

Despite the fact that the series was a science fiction melodrama, there was a conscious effort to maintain credibility.

ALAN ARMER

Shows that work are those where you get involved with people. Most sci-fi series at that time were so far out, the characters were not real people. If the surroundings are too bizarre you dissociate. Not something you become a part of. We strove not to do a comic strip that relied on gimmicks. We had a little bit, because when you got into the environment of the aliens, you couldn't divorce them from it; but we couldn't let that become the show.[2]

DAVID RINTELS
(Associate Producer 1967–1968)

What I always liked about the series was that it tried to put into work stories that had believable characters and situations. The science fiction aspect was the device, but within that, the idea was to have as much credibility as possible concerning people that were recognizable and identifiable. We tried very hard to keep things plausible and highlight as much as possible the real dilemmas of those people involved in the story.[7]

ROBERT DAY
(Director: "The Miracle" *and* "The Peacemaker")

The storylines were fairly relevant without an abundance of special effects. That was what made the series different from other science fiction series on the air in the late 1960s. The Quinn Martin organization was top-notch, and everything they did was quality. Quinn knew exactly the kind of show he wanted and he got it. If not, he'd shoot it again.[8]

Unlike today in episodic television where each series has a staff of in-house writer/ producers, *The Invaders'* producers depended heavily on outside writing.

DAVID RENTILS

Alan (Armer) and I would meet with the freelance writers that we gave assignments to, and give them notes that we all agreed upon. The challenge was to get a steady supply of "A-level" scripts from these writers and hope that we got back quality work that we could rewrite/ polish in time for the director to prepare and then begin shooting.[7]

Ironically, not too many of the freelance writers hired to write episodes were well-versed in science fiction, and those that were proved unable to grasp what was needed.

ALAN ARMER

Some of our really good writers couldn't wrap their minds around a concept that in their heart of hearts they found difficult to believe in. As a result, it became a job for Tony (Spinner) David Rintels (who joined us for season two) and me to breathe life into lukewarm material, giving it the humanity and believability it needed. As a producer, you want every script to be superb. You want the series to be all that you originally conceived it might be. However, it was a challenge to come up with a new script every seven days, meet our scheduled deadlines, and do so in a manner consistent with quality.[2]

On one occasion during season two, a writer was unable to deliver his assigned script which created a difficult situation for the producers. Fortunately, George Eckstein who had written a number of scripts for the Quinn Martin organization was available to help solve the problem.

DAVID RINTELS

George was a fine writer and as professional as they come. We had only several days to come up with a finished result, so we sat down and discussed the story in detail. George wrote two acts, I did two. He rewrote some of mine. I rewrote some of his, then we knitted it together. The show was called "The Trial" and it worked. In fact, it turned out to be one of the best second season episodes.[7]

"The Trial" benefited the series in more ways than one.

HOWARD ALSTON
(Production Manager, 1967–1968)

About the time we were getting ready to prepare for "The Trial," we had budgetary concerns. David and George came up with the idea that much of the story would take place in a courtroom which we built on a stage. That saved us the time and expense of location shooting as well as building other sets.[9]

Another ingredient that helped create attention for *The Invaders* was its weekly guest cast.

HOWARD ALSTON

Casting top-notch actors to guest star was Quinn Martin's trademark. Dating back to *The Untouchables*, he would bring actors out from New York to do the series, pay them "top of the show" and more than any other series in town. As a result, actors loved to work for Quinn. It was one of the reasons for the success of *The Untouchables* and *The Fugitive*.[9]

WILLIAM HALE
(Director: Multiple Episodes)

Quinn Martin and his head casting director John Conwell, were always on the lookout for very talented people. I recall a young actor they had cast as a guest lead in an episode I was directing. One day on the set, he was telling me about a film he had just finished and he encouraged me to see it when it came out. The film was *Bonnie and Clyde*, and the actor's name was Gene Hackman.[10]

Joining Roy Thinnes throughout the series run were Burgess Meredith, Ralph Bellamy, Roddy McDowall, Barbara Hershey, Michael Rennie, Kevin McCarthy, Dana Wynter, Jack Lord, Susan Strasberg, James Whitmore, Ed Begley, Shirley Knight, Louis Gossett, Jr., Jack Warden, James Daly, Suzanne Pleshette, Charles Drake, Anne Francis, Dabney Coleman, Karen Black, Kent Smith, Carol Lynley, Barry Morse, Diane Baker, Peter Graves, Will Geer, Arthur Hill, Antoinette Bower, Pat Hingle, Susan Oliver, Don Gordon, Diana Hyland, Norman Fell, Edward Andrews, William Windom, Edward Asner, Dawn Wells, R. G. Armstrong, Laura Devon, Roscoe Lee Browne, Sally Kellerman, John Larch, Frank Overton, Lynda Day George, Jeanette Nolan, Peter Mark Richman, Barbara Luna, Joseph Campanella, J. D. Cannon, Wayne Rogers, Lynn Loring, Carol Rossen, Fritz Weaver and Alfred Ryder.

Seventeen episodes were broadcast during an abbreviated first season as the show debuted in January.

MARSHALL SCHLOM
(Script Supervisor)

We worked very long hours on *The Invaders*. Sometimes 14-16 hours a day and especially when we did night shooting. In the late 1960s, the turnaround time for the crew (to return to the set) was eight hours. Eventually the unions began to rethink and revise the work hours, and Hollywood changed accordingly.[5]

HOWARD ALSTON

We filmed all over Southern California from the desert to the sea. We shot each episode in seven days, and averaged five days on location and two at the studio. Quinn preferred to not build sets and opted for the realism of real life locations. The various storylines took David Vincent to different parts of the country but we always found what we needed within two hours of Los Angeles. On many a weekend, I would drive all over to find locales that would duplicate our scripted locations.

For example, the episode "Nightmare" supposedly took place in Grady, a small agricultural town in Kansas. We filmed it in Chino, a little town with rolling countryside, and dairy farms, about one hour east of Los Angeles. "Panic" was set in a rural mountain area of West Virginia and we shot that segment in Ojai, a location with pine trees and open meadows about 80 miles northwest of the studio. "Summit Meeting, Part Two" took place in Europe in a mountainous stronghold near the Baltic Sea where a launching would take place. For that location we found a former government missile silo (that had been privatized) in a mountainous area of Palmdale (the high desert) called Fry Canyon about 75 miles north of Los Angeles.[9]

STEPHEN BOWIE
(TV Historian)

In "The Innocent" director Sutton Roley uses wide-angle lenses and bleary soft-focus to create an unworldly look to the aliens' faux paradise, which was actually the picturesque Rossmore Leisure World, a home for the retired in Laguna Hills, California.[11]

PAUL WURTZEL
(Assistant Director)

In a number of our shows we used some offbeat backgrounds, which fit the clandestine activity of the aliens. For one episode, we shot in the Hyperion Sewer Plant below LAX by the ocean. We even built sets in some of the empty warehouses there. On another occasion we went out to Antelope Valley in the desert where they had some very unusual rock formations.[12]

TOM LOWELL
(Actor: "Dark Outpost"*)*

"Dark Outpost" supposedly took place at a remote army base that the aliens were using to hold a group of us as hostages. So the Quinn Martin organization went out and found an old abandoned military base in the Mojave Desert which was a perfect background. We filmed the episode in the summer and the intense heat contributed to the tension in the storyline. In fact, it got so hot at one point Dawn Wells' sneakers began to melt into the concrete floor.[13]

Night shooting was a frequent occurrence.

HOWARD ALSTON

Quinn would not accept "day for night" shooting. It simply didn't have the same look. While you could make it look like night, the sky was always lighter, and the lights you would normally pick up in the background for windows, shops, cars, and street lights, weren't visible in daylight hours. So we always shot "night for night" which was time-consuming, especially when you worked during the day, then had to wait for nightfall.[9]

There was also the matter of the flying saucer.

PAUL WURTZEL

The only actual flying saucer prop we used was the base of the spaceship and the legs, but it was an ordeal to transport them.[12]

HOWARD ALSTON

We always had problems moving the base of the space ship. It was a real expense and took time to do. We needed several trucks to transport it to the various locations. Then we'd have to use a crane to hoist it up and put it together a day or two in advance, depending on where we were.

Then we'd place a guard on it because people didn't know what it was. Yet it worked very well technically. Once we had everything in position, Darrell Anderson (our special effects photographer) would come out and shoot what we had. He always made sure when we shot toward the saucer that we gave him enough footage for what he had to do in the optical house where he put the rest of the saucer together.

The interior of the saucer was filmed on a stage at Samuel Goldwyn Studios. We had a set for the control room and various sets that housed the regeneration chamber. The control panel and other alien equipment props could be plugged into a nearby electrical source, light up and appear operational. We also built on that stage and an adjacent stage, additional sets according to our needs when impractical to use a real-life location.[9]

A second unit crew would film establishing shots, stationary backgrounds, car run-bys, and moving car backgrounds, which was too time-consuming for the main crew.

Ironically, the classic shot of the alien spaceship landing wasn't filmed quite as it appeared on screen.

CARL BARTH
(Second Unit Director)

We shot the "saucer landing scene" out in the valley on Albertson's Ranch, in an open field (which is now Westlake Village, with a huge lake, golf course, shops and homes). We used a lot of arc lights to brightly illuminate the area and simulate the landing of the flying saucer which was later created by Darrell (Anderson) in the optical house.[14]

The series used a minimal amount of special effects, but the one effect people well remember was the incineration of an alien when he died.

PAUL WURTZEL

Basically we would lock down the camera and shoot the actor (playing the alien) in place. He'd then step out of frame and we'd put down ashes and flash powder in the outlined area where he was and shoot that. The immolation that took place in between was done by Darrell Anderson at the optical house, through a series of dissolves and mats blended with our footage to give the desired effect. Darrell would also place kind of a motion in the ash residue which gave it an interesting detail.[12]

To help establish the foreboding mood music for *The Invaders*, Quinn Martin chose Dominic Frontiere to do the theme and main titles. Frontiere had provided music for *The Rat Patrol*, and various Q.M. Series such as *The F.B.I.* and *Twelve O'Clock High*. Yet it was probably his work on *The Outer Limits* that led Martin to assigning him to do *The Invaders*.

JOHN ELIZALDE
(Post Production Supervisor)

Dominic was a gifted composer and one of the most wonderful melodists I had ever known. He had first worked with Quinn and me on *The New Breed* (1961–1962), a police drama we did with Leslie Nielsen.

Ironically, the theme that Dominic used for *The Invaders* was not an original piece written expressly for the show. It was something that came out of his "musical trunk." He had composed it for an unsold pilot *(The Unknown)* in the early 1960s. However, Quinn and I both felt it was an appropriate piece for the series.[15]

STEPHEN BOWIE

Frontiere received credit for the incidental music in four of the earliest Invader episodes. But in addition to writing original music, the composer used bits and pieces of his earlier *Outer Limits* work. The love theme from "Beachhead" [the pilot] initially appeared in the *Outer*

Limits episode "The Man Who Was Never Born," and a haunting waltz from another segment, "The Forms of Things Unknown" crops up in several early *Invaders*.[11]

DUANE TATRO
(Composer: Second Season)

The musical elements that Dominic created in the pilot became musical tools that we used in subsequent episodes. There was a prevalent music cue that Dominic composed that we called the "oui vay" cue. It occurred during moments of crisis. In this "half step" motif, he'd take one note with some orchestra instruments, then another note a half step below it with other orchestra instruments, that produced this dissonant minor second chord. It could be used in various ways, mixing it delicately into the texture of the music at hand to suggest an impending alien presence even if it wasn't a critical moment.[16]

After Frontiere's departure, Elizalde had a musical library to work from including contributions from Richard Markowitz and Sidney Cutner. In the second season, Elizalde turned to Duane Tatro. As a youth, Tatro had played saxophone with the Stan Kenton Orchestra. After graduating from USC with a degree in musical composition, Tatro studied in Paris with renown classical composer Arthur Honegger. Tatro's contemporary/ classical background fit the nature of the show.

JOHN ELIZALDE

Duane wrote quite a few compositions that were perfect for what we wanted. Duane was twelve-tonal (where a composer uses one or several notes in the 12-note scale and doesn't use them again until he uses the remaining notes in the scale). His work tended to be more cerebral whereas Dominic was more of a melodist.[15]

DUANE TATRO

Dick Markowitz and I had worked together and it was he who recommended me to John Elizalde when he left to do another show. The first episode that I did was "The Saucer" (with Anne Francis and Charles Drake).

At the time, my wife and I lived in an apartment in the San Fernando Valley. I didn't have a piano and couldn't afford one. Nearby was a placed called The Little Red Piano Shop. So I walked in there one day and explained my problem to the owner. He suggested I compose there and he gave me a key to the back door. Every night after closing, I went to his shop and in about a week I wrote the score for "The Saucer."

The second show I did was "The Prophet" (with Pat Hingle and Zina Bethune), that concerned an alien posing as an evangelist. The producers weren't happy with the show after it was put together and put it aside. Once they showed it to me, I came up with an off-beat religious concept that gave the episode an added dimension they hadn't thought of. It helped to make the show work.

Two other shows that were memorable musically for me were "Valley of the Shadow" and "The Spores." I found myself writing with empathy for David Vincent and the guest characters that were in conflict. But in the forefront there was always that element of strangeness and air of apprehension.[16]

Tatro eventually did 6–8 shows during the second season but his music extended well into the remainder of the season.

DUANE TATRO

In those days they used a system called "tracking." That was where they took shows that you had done, extracted cues, put them together and used them for the next show; instead of having every show written by the same composer. So my cues were used extensively in subsequent episodes.[16]

A well-equipped soundstage at Goldwyn Studios was provided for scoring.

DUANE TATRO

The soundstage where we recorded had marvelous acoustics. We had a full orchestra of about 35–40 musicians with wonderful recording engineers. There was about 30–34 minutes of music in a one-hour show so we did two three-hour sessions (one in the morning and another in the afternoon).[16]

Twenty-six episodes were filmed during *The Invaders'* second season which debuted on September 5, 1967. David Rintels joined the series as associate producer replacing Anthony Spinner who left at the end of season one.

STEPHEN BOWIE

Rintels was a young, progressive writer. Under his tenure, *The Invaders* began to tackle some political and social issues of the time. The central character in "The Enemy" was a nurse who had witnessed so much horror in Vietnam that Vincent's aliens paled in comparison. "The Captive" takes place in a Russian Embassy and invokes the specter of the Cold War. "The Prophet" and

"The Miracle" criticize religion, obliquely but cannily. In the former, an alien (Pat Hingle) masquerades as an evangelist, delivering sermons to prepare earthlings for the coming invasion. One character, in the parlance of the times, describes religion as "just another trip." In "The Miracle," a naïve girl (Barbara Hershey) mistakes an alien's death for a sign from God.

"The Vise" rather bizarrely combines alien intrigue with race relations, incessantly referencing the Detroit riots as well as Vietnam. Lacking an appropriate sensitivity toward racial awareness, the invaders make some serious errors when disguising one of their own as a black man. His fictitious background fails to reflect the pre-1950 segregation of the U.S. Army, and worse yet, his palms are just as dark as the rest of his skin. In the funniest moment of the entire series, "a group of indignant ghetto residents assail an alien "cop" who tries to arrest Vincent without first reading him his rights!

Rintels' favorite of his own *Invaders* scripts is "The Peacemaker," a Vietnam allegory that shows the aliens in a much more sympathetic light than usual. David Vincent brokers a peace conference between the aliens and the U.S. military. Surprisingly, both the aliens and Vincent himself reluctantly concede that an armistice between the two species could be possible. The truce falls apart not due to alien treachery, but because of the crazed actions of a war mongering general (James Daly) who tries to drop a nuke on the alien leaders who emerge for the negotiations.[11]

Filming the series could create a fair share of attention regardless of whether the invaders were fictitious characters. In the finale of "The Spores," David Vincent throws a Molotov cocktail into a greenhouse full of alien spores, causing an explosion.

WILLIAM HALE

When we scouted the greenhouse location we used for that climactic scene, it was out in the San Fernando Valley, but we didn't notice the proximity to Interstate 5. The effects man rigged a tremendous charge so when the explosion occurred, all hell broke loose. We could hear brakes screeching along with horns blasting and various other noises. When we looked over at the freeway, traffic was stopped and backed up for miles. This was at night, and people must have thought "War of the Worlds" had started.[10]

JOHN ELIZALDE

We wanted a specific sound for the spores when they began to mushroom in the greenhouse scene, but we couldn't put our finger on what we felt was appropriate. Then it came to me. I took a recording of seagulls and played them backward, and it worked.[15]

Midway through season two, David Vincent's one-man crusade to alert the world to the alien invasion ended in "The Believers" episode (telecast December 5, 1967). Vincent was joined by seven allies, some in prominent positions. Now he had contacts capable of helping with research and investigation.

To maintain the identity of the group and the feeling of reality, the character of Edgar Scoville (played by Kent Smith) was introduced. Scoville was the head of an important electronics firm and would be seen in nearly all of the remaining thirteen episodes. Several other members of the group, including Bob Torin (Anthony Eisley) and Army Colonel Archie Harmon (Lin McCarthy) were seen in subsequent episodes, but were killed by the aliens.

The network wanted the change in format because they felt David Vincent's plight seemed such a hopeless one. They believed his task was so huge, that the audience was becoming frustrated and despairing of his success. With only one man against such enormous odds, there was concern the viewer might emotionally turn Vincent off and lose interest. Sharing his problem might open up new areas for exploration and hopefully build new excitement.

In addition, the series moved to a new time on January 9, 1968, from 10 to 11 P.M.

ALAN ARMER

We struggled with the new format and tried to make it work, but the basic truth was my heart wasn't in it. I believed there was a tremendous audience empathy in a single character fighting for his life and the world to believe in something he knew to be true. In part, that was the strength of *The Fugitive* (that I produced for three seasons) and potentially the strength of *The Invaders*, which might have been a few years ahead of its time. Regardless, the network's attempt to boost the ratings by introducing this new premise didn't work.[2]

ROY THINNES

When they brought in a team to work with Vincent, there was no longer the Quinn Martin vision of a study in paranoia. Suddenly it altered everything. We lost a sense of Vincent, the characters he encountered and the drama that was inherent in the previous storylines. It became more of an action-oriented series void of ethics and science, replaced with fear and violence.[17]

DON EITNER

Shifting focus from the main character to a group trivialized the conflict of the show. The earlier episodes were appealing because when David Vincent, a solitary figure, made a connection, it was either taken from him or he'd have to leave it. Most of the latter part of season two focused on plot and circumstance instead of exploring the deeper aspects of the characters in a meaningful way.[4]

In the final episode, "Inquisition," Vincent and Scoville uncover evidence that the aliens have built a sonic device capable of eliminating the human race. During their race to stop them, Scoville is seriously wounded and several "believers" are killed. In the epilogue, a federal prosecutor, Andrew Hatcher (Peter Mark Richman) joins the group and the war against the aliens continues.

Over the years, *The Invaders* has aired infrequently in domestic syndication. However, the relevance of the show was well understood by the British and the French. In England, the series has run several times. In France, the show has become a cult classic and maintained a huge following. Every year, a festival takes place where episodes of *The Invaders* are screened in the movie theaters. A 25th Anniversary was celebrated in 1992 and recently a 40th Anniversary in 2007.

ROY THINNES

In Paris they had a three-story cut-out in front of every Virgin megastore [a video chain throughout Europe] showing David Vincent in flight from a UFO. It was awesome.

I recall walking into a theater in Paris in the mid-1980s where an episode was being shown on widescreen projection to a packed house. I was backstage on the other side of the screen in this enormous movie palace as I was there to do a question-and-answer session. The moment the audience saw David Vincent on the screen, they began to bang on their seats and chant "Daveed, Daveed." When Vincent got out of a car and spoke, the audience began to recite his dialog. It was astounding.[6]

STEPHEN BOWIE

The Invaders may not have been cutting-edge science fiction, but it was a beautifully produced and vastly entertaining bit of escapism, a mood piece that still holds up many years later. It directly influenced Quinn Martin's later entries into the genre (the short-lived 1977 anthology *Tales of the Unexpected*, and a 1980 TV movie called *The Aliens Are Coming*) as well as the most important sci-fi media event of the 1990s, the Fox network's wildly popular series, *The X-Files*.

ROY THINNES

I believe if *The Invaders* were shown today, it would be even more relevant than it was when it originally aired. I recently watched a show on NBC about recent UFO sightings mostly here in the States. The network's posture was more positive about these occurrences because of so many witness accounts that make it indisputable. Back in the late '60s, it would have been dismissed as another hoax. I think everyone is ready to believe. I spoke to an old friend after the show, who reminded me that the Vatican in 1947 (before the Roswell incident), when asked for their opinion about intelligence in the universe other than ours, replied, "The universe must be teeming with civilization."

Anyone who has ever seen the American Museum of Natural History film that takes us into space, through the Milky Way, and allows us to see the countless galaxies beyond us, has to admit something must be out there. Certainly, we're ready to have an intelligent conversation about the possibility of intelligence other than ours. That would explain our continual space exploration. Otherwise, what are we looking for?[6]

Many feel today that the existence of extraterrestrial beings is undeniable.

ROY THINNES

In Russia, Europe, Australia and South America, as well as the United States and Canada, there have been hundreds of witnesses to these events where formations or one single "mother ship," an enormous structure, is flying over and observing us.

An eminent Harvard psychiatrist treated various people from different parts of the world who claimed to have been abducted by aliens. None of his patients had ever met yet they all related similar details in rcalling their encounter with extraterrestrials. In his book *Abduction* which followed, he drew no conclusions. But as a scientist he stated very simply: "It appears that there is something going on that we need to look into. We don't know what it is; but it's happening. All over the world."[6]

The Invaders en route to planet earth.

The nightmare begins.

"BEACHHEAD"
(The Pilot)

Close to where he first saw the space ship land, David Vincent (Roy Thinnes) confronts a suspicious man named John Brandon (James Ward). Suddenly he begins to glow, Vincent makes an effort to detain him, and Brandon tries to kill him. The 90 minute pilot had to be reduced to 60 minutes for network broadcast.

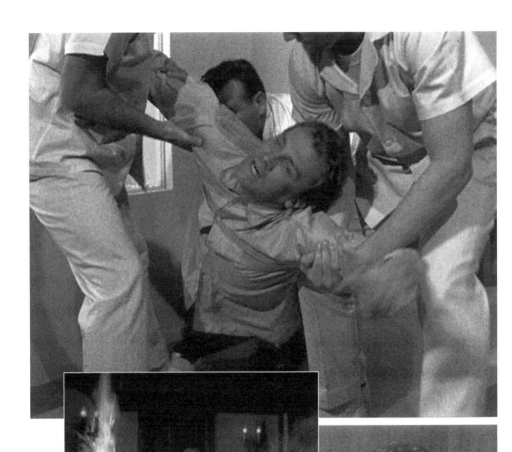

Placed in a sanitarium by his partner Alan Landers and an attending doctor, David Vincent (Roy Thinnes) is later released and discovers a mysterious elderly woman has set fire to his apartment. "Beachhead" was the first of four episodes directed by Joseph Sargent.

Searching for John Brandon in a rural and deserted California town, David Vincent (Roy Thinnes) discovers a regeneration chamber in an abandoned hydro-electric plant; then finds out that Kathy Adams possibly a sympathetic ally, is really inhuman.

Partner Alan Landers (James Daly) arrives at the hydro-electric to help David but encounters two aliens instead. David (Roy Thinnes) finds the body of his friend and partner outside the plant. Sheriff Ben Holman (J. D. Cannon) examines the body and disbelieves David's account of what he saw and what took place. *The Invaders* debuted as a midseason replacement series on Tuesday night, January 10, 1967.

Astrophysicist Curtis Lindstrom has proof of an alien presence and knows they are out to kill him. When that occurs, David Vincent (Roy Thinnes) looks to Lindstrom's son Lloyd for help, unaware that he's controlled by the aliens. "The Experiment" aired January 17, 1967.

David Vincent (Roy Thinnes) is set up by Vicki (Suzanne Pleshette), in reality an alien who has feelings and then tries to save him. "The Mutation" was the third series entry.

The invaders fail to kill David
Vincent and search for him in
the Texas desert. "The Mutation"
was shown January 24, 1967.

Patrolman Hal Corman (Phillip Pine) witnesses an alien revert to his true form and is shocked by what he sees. The after-effect on him involves David Vincent (Roy Thinnes) and police detective Greg Lucather(John Larch). "Genesis" was the fifth episode of season one.

Dr. Ken Harrison (William Sargent, above) is the victim of alien manipulation as they seek to restore one of their own to human form. "Genesis" aired February 7, 1967.

Industrialist George Vikor (Jack Lord) is deluded by alien promises made by alien leader Nexus (Alfred Ryder) in "Vikor," co-starring Diana Hyland.

Knowing Sherri Vikor (Diana Hyland) opposes them, the aliens plan to kill her but George Vikor opposes them.

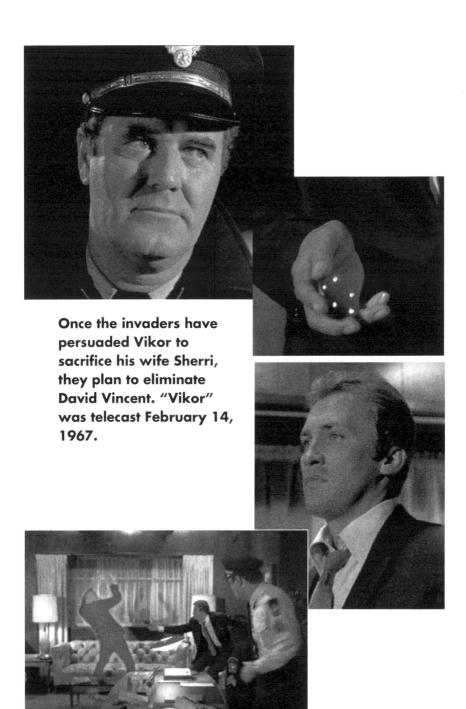

Once the invaders have persuaded Vikor to sacrifice his wife Sherri, they plan to eliminate David Vincent. "Vikor" was telecast February 14, 1967.

In "Nightmare" David Vincent (Roy Thinnes) travels to Grady, Kansas to investigate the claims of a school-teacher, but receives a hostile welcome.

Security guard Harry Swain (James Whitmore) relates his alien vendetta to David Vincent (Roy Thinnes) in "Quantity: Unknown," telecast March 7, 1967.

Scientist Diane Oberly (Susan Strasberg) is reluctant to help David Vincent (Roy Thinnes) in "Quantity: Unknown," episode nine of season one.

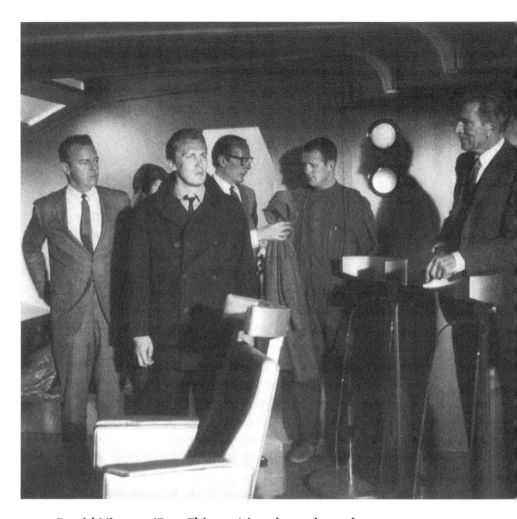

David Vincent (Roy Thinnes) is taken aboard an invader's spacecraft by alien leader Magnus (Michael Rennie) for a special journey in "The Innocent," on March 14,1967.

When Magnus (Michael Rennie) fails to manipulate David Vincent (through mind control) he takes another tactic in "The Innocent," the tenth episode of season one.

In Florida, David Vincent (Roy Thinnes) uncovers an alien conspiracy to unleash a series of hurricanes aimed at destroying major cities along the east coast in "Storm," on April 4, 1967.

David Vincent (Roy Thinnes) attempts to capture an alien with a virus before he's killed by his fellow race in "Panic," April 11, 1967.

David Vincent (Roy Thinnes) persuades sister-in-law Grace Vincent (Julie Sommars) to not contact police when aliens kidnap his brother Robert (Linden Chiles) in "Wall of Crystal," co-starring Burgess Meredith, on May 2, 1967.

David Vincent (Roy Thinnes) boards a flying saucer.

Industrialist Morgan Tate (Ralph Bellamy) learns the invaders have leased his telecommunications facility and his life is then place in jeopardy in "Condemned."

When the aliens fail to kill Morgan Tate and he goes into hiding, they frame David Vincent for his murder. "Condemned" was the seventeenth episode and season one finale on May 9, 1967.

David Vincent (Roy Thinnes) is briefed by Captain Chester Albertson (Forrest Compton) in "Condition Red," the premier episode of season two on September 5, 1967.

David Vincent (Roy Thinnes) and Captain Burt Connors (Burt Douglas) watch a potential confrontation between Air Force jets and an alien spaceship in "Condition Red," guest starring Antionette Bower and Jason Evers.

David Vincent (Roy Thinnes) removes an alien disc from a captured spacecraft as evidence of their presence in "The Saucer," aired September 12, 1967.

David Vincent (Roy Thinnes) descends from a spacecraft and has the drop on two approaching strangers in "The Saucer," the second segment of season two.

Annie Rhodes (Anne Francis) is a woman in flight whose arrival complicates matters for David Vincent (Roy Thinnes) in "The Saucer," co-starring Charles Drake and Dabney Coleman.

David Vincent (Roy Thinnes) encounters Maggie Cook (Shirley Knight) the blind niece of electronics expert Paul Cook (Kevin McCarthy) whom the aliens plan to kidnap and replace with an imposter in "The Watchers" shown September 19,1967.

Alien Joe
Manners (right)
immolates after
being shot by a
sheriff's deputy
in "Valley of
the Shadow,"
on September
26th, 1967.
Below, residents
of Cartersville,
Wyoming
witness his
incineration
which spells
doom for the
entire town.

David Vincent (Roy Thinnes) struggles with Blake (Richard Anderson) the lone survivor of an alien spaceship crash in "The Enemy," on October 3, 1967.

Blake begins to revert to his original alien form in the finale of "The Enemy," co-starring Barbara Barrie.

Charlie Gilman (Don Gordon) an old war buddy of David Vincent (Roy Thinnes) is tried for the murder of a co-worker who in reality was an alien in "The Trial," shown October 10, 1967.

Tom Jessup (Gene Hackman) has a metal case of alien spores that David Vincent wants in "The Spores," broadcast October 17, 1967.

David Vincent (Roy Thinnes) and Steve (Tom Lowell) are held captives by aliens posing as the military in "Dark Outpost," October 24, 1967.

Eileen Brown (Dawn Wells) and Vern Corbett (Andrew Prine) are former lovers adding to the conflict of the captive group in "Dark Outpost."

David Vincent (Roy Thinnes) and Mike Tressider (William Windom) attempt to foil an alien plot to assassinate world leaders in "Summit Meeting, Part Two," telecast November 7, 1967.

David Vincent (Roy Thinnes) is at odds with Sam Crowell as a result of a clever alien scheme involving imposters, diversion, witness intimidation and manipulation in "Labyrinth," that aired November 21, 1967.

In "The Captive"a biochemist (Dana Wynter) in a Soviet embassy determines a burglar may not be human and sends for David Vincent (Roy Thinnes). However, the deputy ambassador believes the man is linked to a possible U.S. warfare project and refuses to hand him over to U.S. military intelligence.

Resourceful electronics industrialist Edgar Scoville (Kent Smith) joins David Vincent (Roy Thinnes) in his war against the invaders in "The Believers" on December 5, 1967.

Elyse Reynolds (Carol Lynley) is a prisoner of the aliens who helps David Vincent (Roy Thinnes) escape but arouses his suspicion in "The Believers."

Edgar Scoville (Kent Smith), David Vincent (Roy Thinnes) and Joan Surrat (Ahna Capri) observe two captured aliens in "Counterattack," on January 9, 1968.

Sarah Concannon (Phyllis Thaxter) with husband General Sam Concannon (James Daly) whose radical beliefs result in family tragedy in "The Peacemaker," the 21st episode of season two.

General Sam Concannon (James Daly) out to bomb a meeting between top alien leaders and key military officials is intercepted by an alien spacecraft in "The Peacemaker," on February 6, 1968.

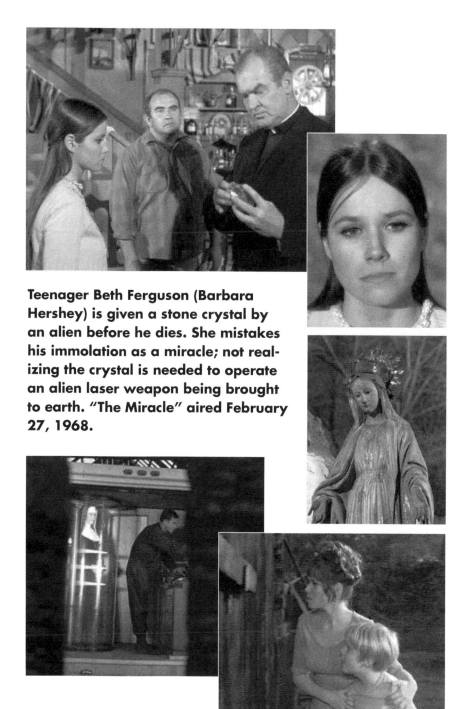

Teenager Beth Ferguson (Barbara Hershey) is given a stone crystal by an alien before he dies. She mistakes his immolation as a miracle; not realizing the crystal is needed to operate an alien laser weapon being brought to earth. "The Miracle" aired February 27, 1968.

Keith (Barry Morse) a fugitive alien opposed to the earth invasion, is aided by David Vincent in "The Life Seekers," shown March 5, 1968.

David Vincent (Roy Thinnes) attempts to get Anne Gibbs (Suzanne Pleshette) an alien, to Washington D.C. to testify before the invaders destroy her in "The Pursued," March 19, 1968.

David Vincent (Roy Thinnes) and Edagr Scoville (Kent Smith) brief Senator Breeding that a high level technical advisor may be an alien. Breeding is unreceptive. Shortly afterward, the aliens kill Breeding and manufacture evidence to support a federal prosecutor (Peter Mark Richman), who believes Vincent and Scoville are responsible. "Inquisition" was the 43rd episode and series finale on March 26, 1968.

Director Paul Wendkos at work in the 1960s. Philadelphian Wendkos directed nine episodes during the series run.

Jack Warden (right) and Susan Oliver (below) guest starred as married couple Barry and Stacy Cahill, an opportunistic couple who unknowingly become involved with aliens operating an indoctrination center in "The Ivy Curtain." Oliver returned to guest as reporter Joan Seeley in "Inquisition," the final episode of the series.

Peter Graves portrayed Gavin Lewis, a former astronaut who helps David Vincent uncover an alien conspiracy at a launching site in "Moonshot."

Burgess Meredith (below) as notable columnist Theodore Booth, plans to expose the extraterrestrials despite alien threats to kill David Vincent's brother in "Wall of Crystal."

Kevin McCarthy had the distinction of playing a dual role in "The Watchers," the third episode of season two. He began his lengthy career on the New York stage and later appeared in many films and network television shows.

Gene Hackman appeared in "The Spores" shortly after completing work on the film "Bonnie and Clyde" which earned him an Academy Award nomination for Best Supporting Actor. Hackman went on to win Academy Awards for "The French Connection" and "Unforgiven."

David Vincent (Roy Thinnes) is a lonely figure in the distance as he watches an alien spacecraft take flight after an aborted landing.

THE INVADERS
Broadcast History (1967–1968)

ABC
Tuesday Nights
8:30 P.M. – 9:30 P.M.
January 10, 1967 – January 2, 1968

ABC
Tuesday Nights
10:00 P.M. – 11:00 P.M.
January 9, 1968 – September 17, 1968

The Cast

David Vincent   Roy Thinnes (1967–1968)

Edgar Scoville   Kent Smith (1968)

Introductory Narrator   Hank Simms (1967–1968)

Story Narrator   William Woodson (1967–1968)

THE INVADERS
Season One (1967)

Episode Titles	Air Dates
1. Beachhead	1/10/67
2. The Experiment	1/17/67
3. The Mutation	1/24/67
4. The Leeches	1/31/67
5. Genesis	2/7/67
6. Vikor	2/14/67
7. Nightmare	2/21/67
8. Doomsday Minus One	2/28/67
9. Quantity: Unknown	3/7/67
10. The Innocent	3/14/67
11. The Ivy Curtain	3/21/67
12. The Betrayed	3/28/67
13. Storm	4/4/67
14. Panic	4/11/67
15. Moonshot	4/18/67
16. Wall of Crystal	5/2/67
17. The Condemned	5/9/67

#1. Beachhead

Executive Producer: Quinn Martin
Producer: Alan Armer
Associate Producer: Anthony Spinner
Written by: Anthony Wilson
Directed by: Joseph Sargent

David Vincent, a 33-year-old architect from Santa Barbara, is returning home from a business trip. He turns off onto a desolate country road in search of a diner that turns out to be deserted. In need of rest, he falls asleep at the wheel, and is awakened by a strange noise and bright glowing lights. In the nearby grassy field, he witnesses an incredible sight: the landing of a flying saucer.

Ben Holman, the Santa Barbara County Sheriff, doesn't believe David's story, nor does David's business partner, Alan Landers. When they return to the site, they encounter the Brandons, two young campers on their honeymoon. They neither saw nor heard anything unusual the night before. During the conversation, David notices that John Brandon has a distorted pinky finger.

David later returns to question Brandon who seems weak and in a hurry to leave. David demands to examine his finger and a fight ensues. Brandon begins to glow brightly before he is able to escape and drive off with his wife.

One night in Santa Barbara, David is asleep on his couch. He awakens to find his apartment ablaze and amidst the flames he sees a mysterious elderly woman. David escapes and decides to look for the Brandons. His search leads him to the small California town of Kinney, the discovery of alien activity, the subsequent murder of his partner, and the beginning of a relentless nightmare.

Cast

Roy Thinnes *(David Vincent)*
James Daly *(Alan Landers)*

Diane Baker *(Kathy Adams)*
J. D. Cannon *(Sheriff Ben Holman)*
John Milford *(Deputy Lou Carver)*
Ellen Corby *(Aunt Sarah)*
James "Skip" Ward *(John Brandon)*
Bonnie Beecher *(Mrs. Brandon)*
Vaughn Taylor *(Kemper)*
Mary Jackson *(Nurse)*
Dennis Cross *(Dennis)*
Shirley Falls *(Secretary)*
Charles McDaniels *(Intern)*

#2. The Experiment

Produced by: Alan Armer
Written by: Anthony Spinner
Directed by: Joseph Sargent

In the small town of Covington in western Pennsylvania, David seeks to aid and abet astrophysicist Dr. Curtis Lindstrom. Lindstrom is aware of the invaders and claims to have documented evidence as proof of their existence.

Suspicious and distrustful of all he meets, Lindstrom finally turns to David for help, but is killed in a supposed car accident.

David is able to convince Lindstrom's son Lloyd that the aliens murdered his father, unaware that the extraterrestrials are using mind control to impose their will on Lloyd, who betrays David.

Cast

Roy Thinnes *(David Vincent)*
Roddy McDowell *(Lloyd Lindstrom)*
Laurence Naismith *(Curtis Lindstrom)*
Harold Gould *(Dr. Paul Mueller)*
Dabbs Greer *(Minister)*
Lawrence Montaigne *(Alien #1)*
Soon-Teck Oh *(Houseboy)*
John Ward *(Trooper)*
Willard Sage *(Lt. James)*
Randy Crawford *(Alien #2)*

#3. The Mutation
Produced by: Alan Armer
Written by: David Chandler
Directed by: Paul Wendkos

David travels to the border town of Rosario where reports of glowing lights and strange noises have been reported. Air Force intelligence and news reporters find no evidence. However, when David is mugged and abandoned by two guides in the nearby desert, he spots an alien spacecraft.

Back in town, an interested reporter named Mark Evans saves David from being run over, and introduces him to a stripper named Vikki who also claims to have seen the spacecraft. David persuades Vikki to guide him to where she saw it, supported by Evans who pays her a fee.

Unknown to Vincent, Evans and Vikki are both aliens luring Vincent into a trap. But Vikki becomes conflicted. She develops feelings for David, but doesn't want to betray her fellow aliens.

Cast

Roy Thinnes *(David Vincent)*
Suzanne Pleshette *(Vikki)*
Edward Andrews *(Mark Evans)*
Lin McCarthy *(Fellows)*
Val Avery *(Club Manager)*
Roy Jenson *(Alien #1)*
Rodolfo Hoyos, Jr. *(Miguel)*
William Stevens *(Cobbs)*
Ted Gehring *(Cabbie)*
Tina Menard *(Mama)*
Tony Davis *(Boy)*
Roberto Contreas *(Guide #1)*
Pepe Callahan *(Guide #2)*

#4. The Leeches
Produced by: Alan Armer
Written by: Dan Ullman
Directed by: Paul Wendkos

Warren Doneghan, the highly publicized and knowledge-able head of an important electronics firm, seeks David's help. Doneghan believes that enemy agents are planning to abduct him. Five other highly profiled scientists in the fields of ocean-ography, mathematics, psychology, and military science have all disappeared within the past year.

Vincent proposes that Doneghan allow himself to be abducted, and that he and Tom Wiley (Doneghan's close friend and head of security) will be in close pursuit. To insure their success, Doneghan devises a small electronic tracking device that he wears around his neck in the form of a medal, but things go awry. The aliens prevent David and Tom from following by disabling their car, then find and destroy the tracking device Doneghan wears. Tom doesn't believe they will find Doneghan, blames David for their predicament, and abandons him during their search in a remote part of the desert.

Cast

Roy Thinnes (David Vincent)
Arthur Hill (Warren Doneghan)
Peter Mark Richman (Tom Wiley)
Diana VanderVlis (Eve Doneghan)
Theodore Marcuse (Noel Markham)
Robert H. Harris (Hastings)
Peter Brocco (Millington)
Noah Keen (Psychiatrist)
William Wintersole (Alien in Charge)
Hank Brandt (Man)
Ray Kellogg (Guard)

#5. Genesis
Produced by: Alan Armer
Written by: John W. Bloch
Directed by: Richard Benedict

Rhode Island patrolman Hal Corman stops an old station wagon being driven with one headlight and hears a strange noise coming from the back. He commands Steve Gibbs, the driver, to open the rear, and witnesses the sight of an alien in its true form. The sight leaves him in a state of shock. His incoherent description of something unearthly brings David to Newport General Hospital, but he is unable to get any further information from Corman. Corman later dies of a cerebral hemorrhage induced by an alien disc.

Detective Greg Lucather is suspicious of David until he shoots and kills an alien attempting to kill David in the underground garage of his hotel. There they discover the station wagon Hal Corman had stopped, and they trace it to owner Dr. Selena Lowell, a research scientist at the Newport Sea Lab. It is there they discover aliens utilizing power to regenerate and return to human form one of their own who is posing as the head of the sea lab.

Cast

Roy Thinnes *(David Vincent)*
John Larch *(Detective Greg Lucather)*
Carol Rossen *(Dr. Selena Lowell)*
Frank Overton *(Grayson)*
Tim McIntire *(Steve Gibbs)*
William Sargent *(Dr. Ken Harrison)*
Phillip Pine *(Hal Corman)*
Jonathan Lippe *(Kevin Ryan)*
Louise Latham *(Joan Corman)*
Bill Erwin *(Manager)*

#6. Vikor

Produced by: Alan Armer
Written by: Michael Adams
Directed by: Paul Wendkos

In Fort Scott, Florida at the Vikor industrial complex, Hank, a telephone lineman witnesses an alien undergoing regeneration to maintain human form. Hank is spotted by Nexus, the alien in charge and flees the scene. Hank later dies of a heart attack and a police investigation finds no evidence to support his story.

A newspaper account brings David to Florida to investigate. He goes undercover as a chauffeur to Sherri Vikor, the lonely, unhappy wife of industrial head George Vikor, to gather evidence of an alien presence.

George, an embittered Korean War hero is collaborating with the invaders by manufacturing regeneration tubes in exchange for enormous wealth and power once the aliens establish themselves. David is able to convince George that the aliens will kill Sherry and double-cross him. George agrees to help David and contact the F.B.I., but ultimately is deluded by alien promises, betrays David and agrees to sacrifice his wife.

Cast

Roy Thinnes *(David Vincent)*
Jack Lord *(George Vikor)*
Diana Hyland *(Sherri Vikor)*
Alfred Ryder *(Nexus)*
Richard O'Brien *(Police Sergeant)*
Joe DiReda *(Phil)*
Hank Simms *(Edward McKendry)*
Sam Edwards *(Hank)*
Hal Baylor *(Guard #1)*
Max Kleven *(Guard #2)*
Larry Duran *(Houseboy)*

#7. Nightmare

Produced by: Alan Armer
Written by: John Kneubuhl
Directed by: Paul Wendkos

In the small agricultural town of Grady, Kansas at the Danielson farm, schoolteacher Ellen Woods sees Constable Gabbard, Ira Danielson and his son Fred operating a strange metallic box with multiple dials and a revolving antenna that emits a strange noise. Fred chases Ellen from their barn, and shortly after she is pursued and attacked by a swarm of carnivorous locusts.

David reads of Ellen's experience and comes to Grady. He's met by a host of unreceptive townspeople including Ellen who is reluctant to discuss her experience. After Ellen's boyfriend Ed Gidney and two others assault David at a lunch counter, Constable Gabbard and his deputy escort David out of town where they try to kill him on a deserted highway.

David escapes and uncovers an alien conspiracy to unleash signal vibrations simultaneously nationwide to trigger a devastating attack by millions of insects including some which are carnivorous.

Cast

Roy Thinnes *(David Vincent)*
Kathleen Widdoes *(Ellen Woods)*
Robert Emhardt *(Oliver Ames)*
Jeanette Nolan *(Miss Havergill)*
James Callahan *(Ed Gidney)*
William Bramley *(Constable Gabbard)*
Irene Tedrow *(Clare Lapham)*
Nellie Burt *(Lena Lapham)*
William Chalee *(Ira Danielson)*
Logan Field *(Carl Gidney)*
John Harmon *(Cook)*
Wayne Heffley *(Deputy)*
Jim Halferty *(Fred Danielson)*
Carey Lofton *(Hank Braden)*

#8. Doomsday Minus One
Produced by: Alan Armer
Written by: Louis Vittes
Directed by: Paul Wendkos

Major Ric Graves, in charge of security at the U.S. Proving Grounds in Utah, contacts David through Charlie Spence who is subsequently killed by the aliens. Graves suspects alien activity on the base, but needs an independent investigator to furnish proof. A significant atomic test will take place soon, so Graves arranges for David to be given a job as a civilian employee.

David uncovers an alien plot involving General Beaumont, the commanding officer on site. The plan: to detonate an anti-matter bomb during the atomic bomb test that could throw the earth off its axis and cause chaos.

Cast

Roy Thinnes *(David Vincent)*
William Windom *(Ric Graves)*
Andrew Duggan *(General Beaumont)*
Wesly Addy *(Tomkins)*
Tom Palmer *(Spence)*
Lee Farr *(Agent)*
Lew Brown *(Officer)*
K. L. Smith *(Guard #1)*
Rick Murray *(Parking Attendant)*
Don Kennedy *(Guard #2)*
Dave Armstrong *(M.P.)*

#9. Quantity Unknown
Produced by: Alan Armer
Teleplay by: Don Brinkley
Story by: Clyde Ware
Directed by: Sutton Roley

A small, weightless cylinder (containing detailed plans of an impending alien invasion) is found at the site of a private plan crash, with no trace of victims. A mail truck carrying the cylinder is robbed by two aliens and two security guards are killed.

David informs A. J. Richards, the head of Sperrick Laboratories, where the cylinder is being analyzed, that relentless enemy agents will try to gain possession of it at all costs. He convinces Richards to set a trap so that they can capture the perpetrators.

A duplicate is made by scientist Diane Oberly and taken to the airport. The aliens are poised to snatch it but pick up on the surveillance and back off. David appears foolish and Richards dismisses him. So do the police.

David is then approached by security guard Harry Swain, a strangely intense man with a vendetta against the aliens. Harry claims to have a friend in military intelligence, so they decide to steal the cylinder and take it to Washington. However, Harry appears desperate and willing to kill anyone that stands in his way, for reasons unclear to David.

Cast

Roy Thinnes *(David Vincent)*
James Whitmore *(Harry Swain)*
Susan Strasberg *(Diane Oberly)*
William Talman *(Frank Griffith)*
Milton Selzer *(A. J. Richards)*
Barney Phillips *(Walt Anson)*
Douglas Henderson *(Lt. Farley)*
Byron Keith *(Air Crash Investigator)*
Ernest Sarracino *(Leo Rinaldi)*

Michael Harris *(Mail Truck Driver)*
Raymond Guth *(Guard #2)*
Melville Ruick *(Minister)*
Ron Doyle *(Rescuer)*

#10. The Innocent
Produced by: Alan Armer
Teleplay by: John W. Bloch
Story by: Norman Klenman, Bernard Rothman
& John W. Bloch
Directed by: Sutton Roley

At Clement Air Force Base, Captain Mitchell Ross is gathering files for an upcoming appearance before a committee investigating UFOs. Late one night, Ross is approached by a suspicious-looking M.P. at gunpoint. Ross manages to fire first and watches his antagonist incinerate.

Ross then summons Vincent to Washington and wants him to testify. David wants to include Nat Greeley, a Maine fisherman who claims to have seen the aliens and possesses one of their weapons—a metallic disc. Ross discounts Greely as the town drunk, but David persuades Ross to allow him to return to Maine, retrieve the disc and bring Greely to Washington.

Greely agrees to give David the disc, but two aliens blackmail him to give it up along with David by threatening the lives of his wife Edna and son, Nat, Jr. Once the aliens capture David, he is delivered to Magnus, a civilized and somewhat charming alien leader who provides a different alien perspective to benefit mankind. To illustrate his point, he takes David aboard their spacecraft on a journey to idyllic St. Margaretta Valley, a place David once dreamed of developing. However, David soon realizes not everything is what it seems to be.

Cast

Roy Thinnes *(David Vincent)*
Michael Rennie *(Magnus)*
William Smithers *(Nat Greely)*
Patricia Smith *(Edna Greely)*
Dabney Coleman *(Captain Mitchell Ross)*
Katherine Justice *(Helen)*
Robert Doyle *(Sgt. Walter Ruddell)*
Paul Carr *(Billy Stears)*
Frank Marth *(Alien #1)*
Harry Lauter *(Alien #2)*
Johnny Jensen *(Nat, Jr.)*
Erik Holland *(Alien M.P.)*

#11. The Ivy Curtain

Produced by: Alan Armer
Written by: Don Brinkley
Directed by: Joseph Sargent

David follows William Burns, an alien posing as an educator/ administrator to the Midlands Academy in Cameron, New Mexico. Vincent infiltrates the school and finds it to be an indoctrination center for newly-arrived aliens. They are taught to act like humans and simulate their emotions, using fear as a weapon, twisting anxiety into hate, suspicion into violence, and cowardice into surrender. All this will contribute to the inevitable destruction of the human race.

Meanwhile, Barney Cahill, a licensed pilot, is unaware of the alien presence and agrees to fly in new recruits to the Academy for a lucrative salary. This enables him to hold onto his young and greedy wife Stacy.

David convinces Barney that his employers are dangerous and persuades him to fly the next group to his own hangar where he'll have police waiting. Stacy, afraid of losing their new source of income, tips off the people at Midlands Academy, unaware of whom she is dealing with.

Cast

Roy Thinnes *(David Vincent)*
Jack Warden *(Barney Cahill)*
Susan Oliver *(Stacy)*
David Sheiner *(William Burns)*
Murray Matheson *(Dr. Reynard)*
Barry Russo *(Lt. Alvarado)*
Clark Gordon *(Mr. Nova)*
Byron Morrow *(Gilbert)*
Paul Pepper *(Dispatcher)*
John Napier *(Invader #1)*
Ted Markland *(Invader #2)*
Laurie Mock *(Invader #3)*

#12. The Betrayed

Produced by: Alan Armer
Teleplay by: John W. Bloch
Story by: Theodore Sturgeon & John W. Bloch
Directed by: John Meredyth Lucas

Reports of strange lights and the death of two watchmen, both from cerebral hemorrhages, bring David to the Carver Oil Fields in Houston. He gets a job designing a plant for owner Simon Carver, and at night he patiently watches the skies.

Finally David witnesses a flying saucer land in the Carver fields behind an abandoned oil tanker. After the saucer leaves, he sneaks aboard the tanker, finds elaborate equipment, and extracts a computer tape that may furnish proof of an alien invasion.

The aliens then exploit David's relationship with Susan Carver, Simon's daughter, to retrieve it. Evelyn Bowers, Carver's secretary, is an extraterrestrial who has knowledge of Simon's troubled past, so she blackmails Susan into spying on David and revealing the whereabouts of the tape.

Cast

Roy Thinnes *(David Vincent)*
Ed Begley *(Simon Carver)*
Laura Devon *(Susan Carver)*
Nancy Wickwire *(Evelyn Bowers)*
Norman Fell *(Neal Taft)*
Bill Fletcher *(First Alien)*
Victor Brandt *(Joey Taft)*
Ivan Bonar *(Older Alien)*
Joel Fluellen *(Henry)*
Ron Stokes *(Alien Technician)*
Gil Stuart *(Waiter)*
Garrison True *(Doctor)*
Max Kleven *(Third Alien)*

#13. Storm

Produced by: Alan Armer
Written by: John Kneubuhl
Directed by: Paul Wendkos

A suspicious pattern of hurricanes have occurred along the Florida coast in mid-February, yet spared the coastal fishing village of St. Matthew. This arouses the curiosity of meteorologist Ed Gantley, as well as David Vincent.

Gantley motors out to inspect the "Lydia J" a small fishing boat at sea that has strangely escaped damage. He finds equipment he has never seen before and is murdered by an alien on board. The invaders have set up a control panel in the town church which regulates equipment on the boat, shooting rays into the atmosphere and triggering storm activity.

David investigates the church, is attacked by two aliens and suffers a concussion. While recuperating at Father Corelli's house, Davis is drugged by the housekeeper Lisa, an alien. Meanwhile her collaborators continue to unleash a series of hurricanes aimed at destroying many of the major cities along the east coast.

Cast

Roy Thinnes *(David Vincent)*
Joe Campanella *(Father Joe Corelli)*
Barbara Luna *(Lisa)*
Dean Harens *(Dr. Leven)*
Carlos Romero *(Luis Perez)*
John McLiam *(Hotel Clerk)*
Paul Comi *(Danny)*
Simon Scott *(Ed Gantley)*
Edward Faulkner *(Alien)*
John Mayo *(Weatherman)*
Allen Emerson *(Organist)*

#14. Panic

Produced by: Alan Armer
Written by: Robert Sherman
Directed by: Robert Butler

In a rural area of West Virginia, Nick Baxter, a young and innocent-looking alien, has a deadly virus which causes those he touches to freeze to death. David traces Nick Baxter's trail and is able to capture him at gunpoint. En route to the Sheriff's office, David is pursued by two aliens out to kill Nick to avoid drawing attention to their activity on earth.

David and Nick encounter Madeline Flagg and her father Gus in a wilderness area. David pays Gus to go off and call the police, leaving Madeline, David and Nick to wait. It is then Madeline begins to show her resentment toward David and sympathy for Nick, unaware of who he is and the disastrous consequences she will bring upon her father.

Cast

Roy Thinnes *(David Vincent)*
Robert Walker, Jr. *(Nick Baxter)*
Lynn Loring *(Madeline Flagg)*
R. G. Armstrong *(Gus Flagg)*
Len Wayland *(Deputy Wallace)*
Ross Hagen *(Wallace)*
Ford Rainey *(George Grundy)*
Rayford Barnes *(Deputy)*
Robert Sorrells *(Station Attendant)*
Joseph Perry *(Joe Bagely)*
Helen Kleeb *(Molly)*
Don Eitner *(Webster)*
Don Ross *(Ed Larson)*
Mercedes Shirley *(Woman Attendant)*
Ralph Thomas *(Deputy in Charge)*

#15. Moonshot
Produced by: Alan Armer
Teleplay by: John W. Bloch & Rita Lakin
Story by: Rita Lakin
Directed by: Paul Wendkos

Clifford Banks and Lt. Colonel Howell are two astronauts slated to participate in a moon launch. While vacationing on board a small fishing boat off the Florida Keys, Banks and Howell are killed by a mysterious red fog.

When David arrives in Florida to investigate, he finds an ally in Gavin Lewis, head of security for the moon launch. Lewis, a former astronaut, washed out of the program after experiencing a sudden case of amnesia and resulting high blood pressure which he has never been able to resolve. David believes the answer lies at the launch site.

Together David and Gavin uncover a conspiracy where the aliens have substituted astronaut Hardy Smith with one of their own.

Cast

Roy Thinnes *(David Vincent)*
Peter Graves *(Gavin Lewis)*
Joanne Linville *(Angela Smith)*
John Ericson *(Hardy Smith)*
Kent Smith *(Stan Arthur)*
Anthony Eisley *(Tony LaCava)*
Richard X. Slattery *(Riley)*
Paul Lukather *(Correll)*
Strother Martin *(Charlie Coogan)*
John Lupton *(Banks)*
Robert Knapp *(Howell)*
Ross Elliott *(McNally)*
John Carter *(Owens)*
Charles McDaniels *(Roberts)*
Steve Cory *(Attendant)*
Morgan Jones *(Reporter #1)*

#16. Wall of Crystal

Produced by: Alan Armer
Teleplay by: Dan Ullman
Directed by: Joseph Sargent

On a deserted California highway, two newlyweds swerve to avoid hitting a pick-up truck carrying chemicals. The truck overturns and the couple watch the driver stumble out and immolate. When they both venture near the truck they die from suffocation after being exposed to crystal clusters that have spilled from a small canister.

David suspects alien activity linked to the accident and drives to the site where it occurred. He finds a crystal cluster in the dirt, begins to suffocate, backs away, then carefully retrieves it in a plastic bag.

Vincent approaches Theodore Booth, a notable TV/ newspaper columnist. Booth agrees to have the crystal analyzed once he's affected by it. He's further motivated when the aliens try to kill him, and David rescues him.

The clusters are used by the aliens to replace oxygen in the air to make the atmosphere more suitable for them and eliminate the need for periodic regeneration.

The invaders then kidnap David's brother, Dr. Robert Vincent, and threaten to kill him unless David recants all of his claims of an alien invasion and prevents Booth from going public. Booth, however, is not willing to cooperate and plans to expose the extraterrestrials.

Cast

Roy Thinnes *(David Vincent)*
Burgess Meredith *(Theodore Booth)*
Linden Chiles *(Dr. Robert Vincent)*
Julie Sommars *(Grace Vincent)*
Edward Asner *(Taugus)*
Lloyd Gough *(Joe McMullen)*
Russ Conway *(Detective Harding)*

Jerry Ayres *(Groom)*
Peggy Lipton *(Bride)*
Mary Lou Taylor *(Mrs. Endicott)*
Ray Kellogg *(Policeman)*
Karen Norris *(Miss Johnson)*

#17. The Condemned

Produced by: Alan Armer
Written by: Robert Sherman
Directed by: Richard Benedict

Morgan Tate leases his Peninsula Telecommunications Laboratory to a company led by Lewis Dunn, unaware they are aliens
using the lab as a nerve center to transmit messages from the
mother planet to key alien leaders on earth.

When Tate finds out, he attempts to steal a file containing the identities and locations of the 11 key alien leaders on
earth. Discovered, Tate hides the file in the lab and flees with his
associate Ed Peterson. During a car chase, Dunn and two other
aliens force Tate's pick-up off the road and incinerate it, but Tate
escapes unseen.

A little girl witnesses the truck disintegrate and Tate escape. The news account of her story brings David to Sand Point,
Oregon. Just outside the front gate of the Peninsula Laboratory,
David notices two electrical workers handling live wires unpro-
tected, and jolts of electricity running through them. He's then
attacked by a security guard and the struggle ensues to a nearby

cliff. David is able to toss the guard over the railing and the alien immolates below.

When the police arrive, Dunn and his associate John Finney tell them the man David fought with and killed was Morgan Tate. The police theorize his body washed out to sea so the aliens produce a bruised and battered body they identify as Tate. David is arrested for murder and neither the police nor his lawyer believe his tales of extraterrestrials.

Cast

Roy Thinnes *(David Vincent)*
Ralph Bellamy *(Morgan Tate)*
Marlyn Mason *(Carol Tate)*
Murray Hamilton *(Lewis Dunn)*
Larry Ward *(Detective Carter)*
John S. Ragin *(John Finney)*
Wright King *(Ed Tonkin)*
Garry Walberg *(Detective Reagan)*
Harlan Warde *(Ed Peterson)*
Paul Bryar *(Brock)*
Kevin Burchett *(Paul)*
Gordon Westcourt *(Joey)*
Geoffrey Duel *(Teenager)*
Seymour Cassel *(Cab Driver)*
Stuart Nisbet *(Coroner)*
Debi Storm *(Victoria)*

THE END of Season One

THE INVADERS
Season Two (1967–1968)

Episode Titles	Air Dates
18. Condition: Red	9/5/67
19. The Saucer	9/12/67
20. The Watchers	9/19/67
21. Valley of the Shadow	9/26/67
22. The Enemy	10/3/67
23. The Trial	10/10/67
24. The Spores	10/17/67
25. Dark Outpost	10/24/67
26. Summit Meeting (Part 1)	10/31/67
27. Summit Meeting (Part 2)	11/7/67
28. The Prophet	11/14/67
29. Labyrinth	11/21/67
30. The Captive	11/28/67
31. The Believers	12/5/67
32. The Ransom	12/12/67
33. Task Force	12/26/67
34. The Possessed	1/2/68
35. Counter-Attack	1/9/68
36. The Pit	1/16/68
37. The Organization	1/30/68
38. The Peacemaker	2/6/68
39. The Vise	2/20/68

Episode Titles	Air Dates
40. The Miracle	2/27/68
41. The Life Seekers	3/5/68
42. The Pursued	3/19/68
43. Inquisition	3/26/68

#18. Condition: Red

Executive Producer: Quinn Martin
Produced by: Alan Armer
Associate Producer: David Rintels
Written by: Laurence Heath
Directed by: Don Medford

While riding in the mountains, Laurie Keller loses control of her horse that is spooked by an approaching car. Laurie is thrown and rendered unconscious. The driver of the car, Dr. Frederick Rogers, administers aid but finds no pulse or heartbeat. He calls the State Police and declares Laurie dead. Rogers then sees three strange men bring Laurie back to consciousness. Two of the men force Rogers to a nearby pond and drown him.

A newspaper account of a doctor reporting a woman dead while her husband (a NORAD Air Force Major) later declares her alive, attracts David's attention. Posing as a freelance magazine writer, David gains admittance to NORAD's Combat Operations Center (A Strategic Air Force defense center for the North American continent) which he believes to be a natural target for the invaders.

David suspects Laurie Keller is an alien. In reality, she is using mind control to extract classified information from her husband. Her mission: to allow her fellow aliens to re-program NORAD computer tapes to not pick up approaching alien spacecraft planning to attack the defense center.

Cast

Roy Thinnes *(David Vincent)*
Antoinette Bower *(Laurie Keller)*
Jason Evers *(Major Dan Keller)*
Simon Scott *(Major Peter Stanhope)*
Forrest Compton *(Albertson)*
Mort Mills *(Mr. Arius)*
Robert Brubaker *(General Winter)*
Burt Douglas *(Capt. Connors)*
Roy Engel *(Dr. Frederick Rogers)*

#19. The Saucer
Produced by: Alan Armer
Written by: Dan Ullman
Directed by: Jesse Hibbs

David teams up with John Carter, an unemployed writer who has seen a flying saucer, and claims he can predict the day and place where another will land. In a rocky, remote desert area they spot a flying saucer arrive. Two aliens left to guard the spacecraft spot David and John and attempt to kill them. David and John prevail and board the saucer, unaware a third alien has escaped to warn other invaders in the area.

John goes for help and recruits State Assemblyman Joe Bonning and Sheriff Sam Thorne, but the three are killed by aliens en route. Meanwhile David, who is guarding the saucer, encounters Robert Morrison, an electrical engineer, and his girlfriend Annie Rhodes whose private plane has crashed nearby. Annie believes Robert has stolen valuable blueprint plans from his company and that they have fled intending to reach Mexico. Robert, in reality not a thief, chooses to stay and help David, but Annie, thinking the police are coming, leaves and is captured by approaching aliens, compromising David's possession of their spacecraft.

Cast

Roy Thinnes *(David Vincent)*
Anne Francis *(Annie Rhodes)*
Charles Drake *(Robert Morrison)*
Dabney Coleman *(John Carter)*
Sandy Kenyon *(Alien Leader)*
Kelly Thordsen *(Sheriff Sam Thorne)*
Robert Knapp *(Joe Bonning)*
John Ward *(Alien Pilot)*
Glenn Bradby *(Doctor)*
Tina Menard *(Maid)*
Chris Shea *(Boy)*

#20. The Watchers

Produced by: Alan Armer
Teleplay by: Jerry Sohl & Earl Hamner, Jr.
Story by: Earl Hamner, Jr. & Michael Adams
Directed by: Jesse Hibbs

The manager of a Virginia mountain resort is driven to an apparent suicide on an airplane runway just after claiming that aliens have taken over his hotel.

David arrives at the airport and observes the clandestine arrival of electronics expert Paul Cook and his blind niece Maggie. Cook is scheduled to meet with two top military officials at the resort to upgrade the country's missile defense system.

Working as a bus driver, David discovers an alien plot to replace Cook with a look-alike and gain possession of the country's defense plans.

Cast

Roy Thinnes *(David Vincent)*
Kevin McCarthy *(Paul Cook)*
Shirley Knight *(Maggie Cook)*
Leonard Stone *(Ramsey)*
Robert Yuro *(Simms)*
Walter Brooke *(Danvers)*
Harry Hickox *(Bowman)*
John Zaremba *(General)*
James Seay *(Grayson)*
Paul Sorenson *(Alien #1)*
Marlowe Jensen *(Alien #2)*

#21. Valley of the Shadow
Produced by: Alan Armer
Teleplay by: Robert Sabaroff
Story by: Howard Merill & Robert Sabaroff
Directed by: Jesse Hibbs

Dr. Sam Larousse and his fiancée Dr. Maria McKinley come to the aid of car accident victim Joe Manners who loses control of his car which overturns. Neither doctor realizes that Manners is an alien in need of regeneration. When Maria takes out a stethoscope, Manners panics and tries to flee. When Sam attempts to restrain him, Manners kills him with a rock. Two state policemen arrive before Manners can harm Maria, and they subdue him. Manners is arrested and jailed in the nearby town of Cartersville.

David arrives in the small Wyoming town and identifies Manners as an alien who once tried to kill him. He persuades Sheriff Clements to have a doctor examine Manners and confirm that he has no pulse or heartbeat. Then, David contacts Captain William Taft in Air Force Intelligence to be a witness.

Manners, who pretends to call his lawyer, tips off nearby aliens that Taft is coming. Taft and his driver are intercepted and an alien imposter arrives in his place. When Manners is about to be examined, he flees the jail and is killed in the town square by Clement's deputy. A large number of people witness Manner's immolation.

The alien impersonating Taft declares Marshall Law, then his fellow aliens cut off the town's power to isolate them. But the worst is yet to come. The invaders plan to annihilate the entire town of Cartersville.

Cast

Roy Thinnes *(David Vincent)*
Nan Martin *(Maria McKinley)*
Harry Townes *(Will Hale)*
Ron Hayes *(Sheriff Clements)*
Joe Maross *(Taft)*

Mark Roberts *(Dr. Larousse)*
Hank Brandt *(Joe Manners)*
Ted Knight *(Alien Leader)*
Robert Sorrells *(Deputy)*
Don Eitner *(Townsperson)*
Jon Lormer *(Minister)*
James B. Sikking *(Capt. William Taft)*
Claudia Bryar *(Townsperson #2)*
Phil Chambers *(Townsperson #3)*

#22. The Enemy

Produced by: Alan Armer
Written by: John W. Bloch
Directed by: Robert Butler

In a remote section of southern Utah, Gale Fraser sees a flying saucer crash land behind her property. Blake, the only alien survivor, is in need of regeneration. Gale, a nurse who recently served in Vietnam, is sympathetic to his condition and helps keep him alive by injections of a fluid from vials in his possession.

Blake, distrustful of humans, is on a mission to deliver a courier box containing chemicals for experimentation. The aliens hope to change their chemistry and utilize the earth's oxygen to help them exist.

David has been searching the area after reported UFO sightings and a mysterious crash. He finds the courier box at the crash site and is able to capture a weakened Blake. However, Gale is not a willing ally. She believes the aliens may be here on a mission of peace, and feels they have to defend themselves against the human race which destroys that which they don't understand.

Cast

Roy Thinnes *(David Vincent)*
Barbara Barrie *(Gale Frazer)*
Richard Anderson *(Blake)*
Paul Mantee *(Vern Hammond)*
Gene Lyons *(Sawyer)*
Russell Thorson *(Sheriff)*
George Keymas *(Lavin)*

#23. The Trial

Produced by: Alan Armer
Written by: George Eckstein & David Rintels
Directed by: Robert Butler

In Jackson County, Indiana, Charlie Gilman suspects Fred Wilk, a co-worker at his plant, to be an alien. He informs David, his Korean War buddy, who arrives on the scene.

Wilk suspects Charlie is on to him and attacks him with a pipe wrench in the furnace room. During the fight, Charlie manages to take away the wrench. David and security cop Burt Winofsky arrive but the door is locked. Through an upper screen window, they see Charlie strike Wilk with the wrench. Winofsky shoots out the lock, and when he and David enter, Charlie is standing alone in front of the furnace. Charlie claims Wilk disintegrated, but the police arrest him for murder, claiming Charlie tossed the body into the furnace.

Complicating matters for the defense at the trial are revelations that Wilk was married to Charlie's former fiancée, and that Charlie threatened his life during an altercation.

Cast

Roy Thinnes *(David Vincent)*
Don Gordon *(Charlie Gilman)*
Russell Johnson *(Robert Bernard)*
Lynda Day *(Janet Wilk)*
Harold Gould *(Alan Salter)*
Malcolm Atterbury *(Judge Symondson)*
Bill Zuckert *(Burt Winofsky)*
Richard Hale *(Fred Wilk, Sr.)*
Jason Wingreen *(Clerk)*
Amy Douglass *(Mrs. Wilk)*
John Rayner *(Fred Wilk)*
James McCallion *(Brennan)*

#24. The Spores
Produced by: Alan Armer
Written by: Ellis Kadison & Joel Kane
Story by: Al Ramrus, John Shaner, Ellis Kadison & Joel Kane
Directed by: William Hale

A spaceship lands near Phillipsburg, Colorado, bringing an experimental cargo of 24 spores. When exposed to the earth's atmosphere, each spore will grow into a perfectly formed alien.

Tom Jessup and three other aliens are transporting the spores to an incubation station in a metal case when their truck overturns on a country road. Jessup is the only survivor.

Ernie Goldhaver, a deputy sheriff, sees the crash and witnesses two of the aliens incinerate. A radio newscast of the incident brings David to Phillipsburg. At the crash site David sees Jessup walking away, carrying the metal case. He offers him a ride, and during a stop at a café, David overhears Jessup call another alien. David attempts to steal the suitcase, a fight ensues, and three teens steal it. The suitcase changes hands again, going from a couple down on their luck to a trio of kids, with David and the aliens in close pursuit.

Cast

Roy Thinnes *(David Vincent)*
Gene Hackman *(Tom Jessup)*
Mark Miller *(Jack Palay)*
Patricia Smith *(Sally Palay)*
John Randolph *(Ernie Goldhaver)*
Wayne Rogers *(John Mattson)*
James Gammon *(Hal)*
Judee Morton *(Mavis)*
Kevin Coughlin *(Roy)*
Vince Howard *(Frank)*
Joel Davidson *(Earl Garber)*
Brian Nash *(Mike)*
Steven Liss *(Archie)*
Christine Marchett *(Elizabeth Garber)*

#25. Dark Outpost
Produced by: Alan Armer
Written by: Jerry Sohl
Directed by: George McCowan

David becomes a stowaway aboard an alien spacecraft landing in a remote desert area. There he encounters archeologist John Devin and his students Vern, Eileen, Hal, Steve and Nicole.

The group accompanies him back to the landing site but the flying saucer is gone. David and John Devin find tracks leading from the site and trace them to Camp Crowley, a desolate army base nearby. There they witness diseased aliens being restored to health via a circular-shaped crystal device. David steals the crystal and escapes, but the aliens kill Devin.

Back at the archeological site, David tries to convince the disbelieving students of an alien presence when they are taken into custody and transported to Camp Crowley by a group of aliens posing as an army platoon.

The base commander, Colonel Harris, demands that David return the crystal. When all the men side with David, Harris explains that they are interfering with national security and that everyone in the group is considered an enemy of state. He threatens to execute them, one by one. When he doesn't get satisfaction, he takes Steve out first, but David, Vern, and Eileen all witness a different form of execution.

Cast

Roy Thinnes *(David Vincent)*
Andrew Prine *(Vern Corbett)*
Dawn Wells *(Eileen Brown)*
Tim McIntire *(Hal)*
Tom Lowell *(Steve)*
William Sargent *(Dr. John Devin)*
Kelly Jean Peters *(Nicole)*
Whit Bissell *(Col. Harris)*
Susan Davis *(Mrs. James)*
William Wintersole *(Carr)*

William Stevens *(Sergeant)*
Brad Stevens *(Ambulance Driver)*
Walter Reed *(Major)*
Sam Edwards *(Thatcher)*

#26. Summer Meeting (Part 1)
Produced by: Alan Armer
Written by: George Eckstein
Directed by: Don Medford

Defense contractor Mike Tressider informs David Vincent that the radiation levels in the atmosphere are rising and that in six months most of the planet earth will be unfit for human existence. The exception is a small area of Scandinavia where a rash of UFO sightings have occurred. Tressider believes the aliens are using that corner of the planet as headquarters to destroy the world with radioactivity.

Upcoming is a summit conference of world leaders headed by Scandinavian Premiere Thor Halvorson whose country has researched and manufactured AR5, an anti-radiation pollutant to eliminate the toxic elements in the poisoned air. Halvorson plans to launch AR5 at the conference.

Vincent and Tressider then learn from alien Ellie Markham that the summit is a front for an alien plot to assassinate all of the world leaders and their aides, with aliens waiting in each country to take their places. The missile launching will release a deadly gas (non-toxic to aliens) that will kill all within a ten mile radius.

Cast

Roy Thinnes *(David Vincent)*
Michael Rennie *(Alquist)*
William Windom *(Mike Tressider)*
Diana Hyland *(Ellie Markham)*
Eduard Franz *(Thor Halvorson)*
Ford Rainey *(Jonathan Blaine)*
Martin West *(Lieutenant)*
Ian Wolfe *(Rosmundson)*
Ben Wright *(Emissary)*
Ross Elliot *(Hotel Detective)*
Vic Perrin *(Hypnotist)*
Don Lamond *(Newsman)*
Peter Hobbs *(Colonel)*

#27. Summit Meeting (Part 2)

Produced by: Alan Armer
Written by: George Eckstein
Directed by: Don Medford

At the summit meeting in a mountain stronghold ten miles from the Baltic Sea, Vincent and Tressider work feverishly to expose alien Alquist, Halvorson's trusted aide, and prevent the mass assassination of the world's leaders.

Cast

Roy Thinnes *(David Vincent)*
Michael Rennie *(Alquist)*
William Windom *(Mike Tressider)*
Diana Hyland *(Ellie Markham)*
Eduard Franz *(Thor Halvorson)*
Richard Eastham *(Colonel Vanders)*
Jay Lanin *(Alquist Aide)*
Lew Brown *(Military Aide)*
Hank Simms *(News Narrator)*
Troy Melton *(Journalist #1)*
Lee Farr *(Alien)*
John Mayo *(Alien)*
Albert Carrier *(Frenchman)*
Morgan Jones *(Guard)*
Don Ross *(Journalist #2)*

#28. The Prophet

Produced by: Alan Armer
Teleplay by: Warren Duff
Story by: Jerry DeBono
Directed by: Robert Douglas

David attends an evangelist event and watches Brother Avery prophesy the coming of a heavenly host that will heal our ills and bring peace to mankind. At the climax of his service, Avery begins to glow intensely before being escorted off the stage by two assistants. David follows them outside to a nearby truck with a high voltage power line.

David contacts columnist Bill Shay of NOW Magazine, and offers to get photos of the inside of the truck that will show a regeneration chamber and prove Avery is an alien. To accomplish his task, Vincent poses as a spiritual follower interested in joining the organization as an apprentice. Bill Shay tips off Brother John, Avery's top aide. John tries to kill David but perishes instead.

Vincent then turns to Sister Claire, an important member, who catches him spying. Claire is a disillusioned woman who feels Brother Avery has given her beauty, faith and a reason for living. However, after an emotional confrontation with David, Claire begins to have doubts about Avery which places her life in jeopardy.

Cast

Roy Thinnes *(David Vincent)*
Pat Hingle *(Brother Avery)*
Zina Bethune *(Sister Claire)*
Roger Perry *(Bill Shay)*
Richard O'Brien *(Brother John)*
Byron Keith *(Brother James)*
Dan Frazier *(Reporter)*
Ray Kellogg *(Guard)*

#29. Labyrinth

Produced by: Alan Armer
Written by: Art Wallace
Directed by: Murray Golden

David brings an injured, unconscious alien to the office of Dr. Henry Thorne. His shoulder x-rays reveal no bone structure. Thorne decides to take another, but before he can act, the alien regains consciousness and kills him. During a struggle to prevent the alien from destroying the x-rays, David kills him.

Now armed with potential evidence of an alien existence, David contacts Professor Harrison and Doctor Crowell who head a government research project on UFOs at a prominent Illinois university.

However, David faces a daunting path. The aliens have engineered a cleverly thought-out plan that includes imposters, witness intimidation, discrediting David, and diversion by one of their own close to the research project, which faces an impending deadline to furnish evidence of extraterrestrials on earth.

Cast

Roy Thinnes *(David Vincent)*
Ed Begley *(Sam Crowell)*
Sally Kellerman *(Laura Crowell)*
James Callahan *(Harry Mills)*
Virginia Christine *(Mrs. Thorne)*
Ed Peck *(Darrow)*
Martin Blaine *(Argyle)*
E. J. Andre *(Henry Thorne)*
John Zaremba *(Prof. Ed Harrison)*
William Quinn *(Lt. Eaton)*
Barbara Dodd *(Miss Fox)*
William Sumper *(Cab Driver)*
Wilhelm von Homburg *(Alien Patient)*

#30. The Captive

Produced by: Alan Armer
Written by: Laurence Heath
Directed by: William Hale

A burglar breaks into the Soviet Embassy and is shot by security. Dr. Katherine Serret, a research biochemist on staff, examines the burglar and finds no blood, pulse or heartbeat. Unsure of who or what this man named Sanders really is, Serret sends for David Vincent.

David advises Deputy Ambassador Peter Borke to get Sanders out of the embassy and hand him over to military intelligence or state department security. Despite evidence to the contrary, Borke, a cautious, misguided man, believes that Sanders may be manufactured and linked to a U.S. biological warfare project. He decides to detain David until he can get satisfactory answers.

In the meantime, the aliens cannot risk exposure and must get Sanders out of the embassy. If not, they plan to blow it up and thus create a confrontation between the U.S. and the Soviets.

Cast

Roy Thinnes *(David Vincent)*
Dana Wynter *(Dr. Katherine Serret)*
Fritz Weaver *(Peter Borke)*
Don Dubbins *(Wesley J. Sanders)*
Lawrence Dane *(Josef Dansk)*
Douglas Henderson *(Martin)*
Jock Gaynor *(Connor)*
Tom Palmer *(Dorian)*
Peter Coe *(Leo)*
Dallas Mitchell *(Jim Rogers)*
Robert Patten *(Murphy)*
Alex Rodine *(Guard)*

#31. The Believers

Produced by: Alan Armer
Written by: Barry Oringer
Directed by: Paul Wendkos

A group of people that share David's awareness of the invaders have banded together, headed by Edgar Scoville, the resourceful head of an electronics firm. Upon leaving a clandestine meeting with three allies, David and the group are ambushed by aliens. David, the lone survivor, is kidnapped.

The aliens are aware of the group of believers, and they have become their main target. Under hypnotic interrogation, the extraterrestrials hope to learn the name of David's associates, but he gives them false information.

Just when David is about to be executed, he is rescued by army soldiers and awakens in a military hospital. Col. Newcombe of U.S. Military Intelligence briefs David on their involvement and their priority to gather up the believers and place them in protective custody. But David realizes that his rescue and Newcombe are part of a charade to get him to reveal names.

Next, David meets fellow prisoner Elyse Reynolds, a psychologist who seems anxious to help David and prove she is not an alien. Elyse relates a fantastic plot to be carried out where the aliens attack the major cities by starting fires, floods and power breakdowns. In so doing, they would cut the leadership off from contact with the people and turn every city into a panic-stricken mob. Elyse shows David a way they can escape, but several more believers die and David begins to wonder if his new-found ally is sincere or, for some reason, collaborating with the aliens to reveal the identities of the believers.

Cast

Roy Thinnes *(David Vincent)*
Carol Lynley *(Elyse Reynolds)*
Anthony Eisley *(Bob Torin)*
Kent Smith *(Edgar Scoville)*

Donald Davis *(Harland)*
Rhys Williams *(Prof. Hellman)*
Byron Morrow *(Col. Newcombe)*
Maura McGivney *(Mary Torin)*
Kathleen Larkin *(Lt. Sally Harper)*
Richard Karlan *(Charles Russellini)*
Hal Baylor *(Friendly Guard)*
Mark Tapscott *(Security Guard)*
Allen Emerson *(Library Alien)*
Ed Barth *(Cab Driver)*
Ed Long *(Corridor Guard)*
Tim Burns *(Student)*
Warren Parker *(Arthur Singeiser)*

#32. The Ransom

Produced by: Alan Armer
Written by: Robert Collins
Directed by: Lewis Allen

In the mountains of Harper County, Vermont, at a closed ski lodge, David and ally Bob Torin capture an alien leader about to undergo regeneration. The alien informs them if they don't let him go, there will be a terrible retribution.

Back at their motel, he makes them a final offer: free him and his race will withdraw from their expedition and return to their planet. David is distrustful and motivated to get this very important alien to Washington.

Help is twelve miles away at Camp Belding where Edgar Scoville awaits them. In addition, police are en route to the motel. But four aliens arrive, begin to search the motel and con the police when they arrive.

David and company flee while Bob Torin tries to reach Camp Belding. David with his alien captive, seeks refuge in the mountain home of ailing poet Cyrus Stone and his granddaughter Claudia. However, David has backed himself into a corner. The invaders have surrounded the house, cut the phone lines, killed Bob Torin, and their captured leader has three hours left to live without regeneration.

Cast

Roy Thinnes *(David Vincent)*
Laurence Naismith *(Cyrus Stone)*
Alfred Ryder *(Alien Leader)*
Karen Black *(Claudia Stone)*
Anthony Eisley *(Bob Torin)*
Kent Smith *(Edgar Scoville)*
Lawrence Montaigne *(Garth)*
John S. Ragin *(Kant)*
Christopher Held *(Lieutenant)*
Ron Husman *(Sentry)*
John Graham *(Col. Gentry)*
Joe Quinn *(Policeman)*

#33. Task Force

Produced by: Alan Armer
Written by: Warren Duff
Directed by: Gerald Mayer

The aliens are on a mission to take over the news media. They infiltrate NOW Magazine, a modern day news periodical published by Mace Publications. William Mace, the head of the company, is a curious man with an insatiable thirst for facts. He's intrigued by David and associate editor Bob Ferrera's explanation as to why key executives keep leaving, and who a certain group of people are that keep pressing Mace to buy control of his company.

Mace decides to support David, Edgar Scoville and their group of believers, using all of his resources. An alien task force decides to eliminate Mace and exploit his immature, irresponsible nephew Jeremy Mace, the heir apparent.

The aliens kidnap and kill William Mace, forcing Jeremy to watch, then threaten the lives of all close to him unless he cooperates. Jeremy is then forced to take in the aliens posing as a syndicate that has made a substantial investment in Mace Publications.

Cast

Roy Thinnes *(David Vincent)*
Linden Chiles *(Jeremy Mace)*
Nancy Kovack *(June Murray)*
Kent Smith *(Edgar Scoville)*
Martin Wolfson *(William Mace)*
Frank Marth *(Eric Lund)*
John Lasell *(Bob Ferrera)*
Barney Phillips *(Emmett Morgan)*
John Stephenson *(John Niven)*
Walter Woolf King *(Head Alien)*

#34. The Possessed

Produced by: Alan Armer
Written by: John W. Bloch
Directed by: William Hale

David receives an urgent letter from Dr. Ted Willard, his college roommate. Ted has found evidence of alien experimentation at the New Mexico sanitarium run by him and his brother Dr. Martin Willard. Ted's discovery is thwarted by alien Adam Lane who is supervising a computerized program in behavior control at the sanitarium laboratory. Ted is then subjected to an operation to program his behavior. Martin Willard is collaborating with the invaders. He believes in their superiority and ultimate conquest. Lane has sold him on the idea that if their program is successful, there will be no resistance and millions of lives will be spared.

When David arrives, Ted has no memory of the content of the letter he wrote, but David is aware of Lane and that Martin is a collaborator. Lane is also aware of David, and programs Ted to kill him.

Cast

Roy Thinnes *(David Vincent)*
Michael Tolan *(Dr. Ted Willard)*
William Smithers *(Adam Lane)*
Katherine Justice *(Janet Garner)*
Michael Constantine *(Dr. Martin Willard)*
Kent Smith *(Edgar Scoville)*
Charles Bateman *(Burt Newcomb)*
Booth Coleman *(Coroner)*
Matt Pelto *(Clerk)*
Rose Hobart *(Housekeeper)*
Lyn Hobart *(Alien Nurse)*

#35. Counter-Attack

Produced by: Alan Armer
Written by: Laurence Heath
Directed by: Robert Douglas

The believers take their first offensive action against the invaders. Astronomer Elliot Kramer creates a computerized program that will jam the navigation signals the aliens are using to get from their planet to earth. In causing their guidance system to malfunction, saucers will crash and create public awareness.

When David and Kramer exit the faculty annex of the University where Kramer teachers, they are met at gunpoint by two aliens demanding Kramer's briefcase. A fight ensues and David manages to kill both extraterrestrials. During the struggle, Kramer suffers a fatal fall.

The security guard comes out to find David hovering over Kramer's body. David tells the guard Kramer is dead, to call the police, and rushes off with Kramer's briefcase. David is able to get the program to Edgar Scoville and computer scientist Jim Bryce, but shortly after he's arrested for the murder of Elliot Kramer.

Cast

Roy Thinnes *(David Vincent)*
Lin McCarthy *(Col. Archie Harmon)*
Donald Davis *(Lucian)*
Ahna Capri *(Joan Surrat)*
Kent Smith *(Edgar Scoville)*
John Milford *(Jim Bryce)*
Ken Lynch *(Lt. Connors)*
Pamela Curran *(Louise)*
Warren Vanders *(Earl)*
Don Chastain *(Blake)*
Ross Elliott *(Elliot Kramer)*
Charles Stewart *(Robertson)*
Ed Prentiss *(Stan Leeds)*
Walter Baldwin *(Security Guard)*

#36. The Pit
Produced by: Alan Armer
Written by: Jack Miller
Directed by: Lewis Allen

Professor Julian Reed is a member of David Vincent's believers. Reed is employed at the Slaton Research Center where some of the finest minds have gathered to deal with problems related to the U.S. space program. There is also research and development related to magnetic propulsion [supposedly the source of alien spacecraft].

Julian has been hospitalized for psychotic behavior. His wife, Patricia Reed, also a scientist at the Center, cannot understand her husband's mental breakdown. In the hospital, David finds Julian calm and rational, and his friend relates a disturbing scenario. Julian suspects alien interference at the Center where important projects submitted to the government have been canceled. He knows Jeff Brower, his assistant in dream research, is an alien, and has deliberately induced his hallucinations, paranoia and psychotic episodes through dream deprivation, all in an effort to discredit him.

Cast

Roy Thinnes *(David Vincent)*
Charles Aidman *(Julian Reed)*
Joanne Linville *(Patricia Reed)*
Donald Harron *(Jeff Brower)*
Kent Smith *(Edgar Scoville)*
Simon Scott *(John Slaton)*
Johnny Jensen *(Frankie Reed)*
Bartlett Robinson *(Llewellan)*
Dort Clark *(Security Officer)*
Pat O'Hara *(Scientist)*
Lizabeth Field *(Mrs. Fielding)*
Michael Harris *(Security Guard)*

#37. The Organization

Produced by: Alan Armer
Written by: Franklin Barton
Directed by: William Hale

A flying saucer collides with a weather satellite and crashes in the ocean. A nearby ship gathers up the metal pieces and electrical wiring from the wreckage and stores it in a cargo hold. Columnist Mike Calvin writes up the incident but from the Air Force point of view that a meteor collided with the satellite.

The aliens retrieve their remnants but by mistake confiscate an additional cargo box that contains narcotics belonging to the mob. When David and Mike search for the saucer remains, David falls into the hands of two mobsters. Once the Mafia knows that David was not after their drugs, they let him go. But David chooses to form an alliance with the Organization. He feels their resources will enable him to get back the crate of saucer fragments and possibly uncover good evidence. Edgar Scoville is against their joining a contingent of organized crime. He believes that David will place his life in jeopardy by helping them to get back their narcotics; but David makes the deal.

Ultimately, the aliens meet the Organization and are willing to return their ten million dollar shipment of drugs, but only if the Organization gives up David—dead or alive.

Cast

Roy Thinnes *(David Vincent)*
J. D. Cannon *(Peter Kalter)*
Chris Robinson *(Mike Calvin)*
Larry Gates *(Weller)*
Kent Smith *(Edgar Scoville)*
Roy Poole *(Court)*
John Kellogg *(Dominic)*
Barry Atwater *(Dorcas)*
Ross Hagen *(Perry)*
Nelson Olmstead *(Amos Foster)*
Mark Allen *(Second Mate)*
Troy Melton *(Chauffeur)*

#38. The Peacemaker
Produced by: Alan Armer
Written by: David Rintels
Directed by: Robert Day

David and Colonel Archie Harmon capture an alien and transport him to a military cell in the Washington, D.C. area.

Vance, an alien posing as a junior officer, slips a pill to his compatriot who incinerates after swallowing it. Before Vance can get away, Harmon returns with General Sam Concannon, and they watch the air policeman (who was guarding the cell) shoot Vance, who also incinerates.

Concerned by the alien existence and what they might do, Concannon instructs David to set up a meeting with the invaders to make a responsible settlement, and avoid a war. A meeting is arranged between several important alien leaders and Edgar Scoville, Concannon and several key military officials. But in his zeal to stop the aliens, Concannon plans to drop a bomb on the meeting site, killing everyone there and within a ten mile radius.

Cast

Roy Thinnes *(David Vincent)*
James Daly *(General Concannon)*
Phyllis Thaxter *(Sarah Concannon)*
Lin McCarthy *(Col. Archie Harmon)*
Alfred Ryder *(Alien Leader)*
Kent Smith *(Edgar Scoville)*
Jan Merlin *(Post)*
Pat Cardi *(Billy Concannon)*
Craig Huebling *(Willard)*
Larry Thor *(Dr. Jacobs)*
Byron Keith *(General Cullenbine)*
Jack Bannon *(Vance)*
Ed Deemer *(Air Policeman)*

#39. The Vise

Produced by: Alan Armer
Teleplay by: William Blinn
Story by: Robert Sabaroff & William Blinn
Directed by: William Hale

David and Edgar Scoville find evidence that Afro-American Arnold Warren, being nominated for an important post in the international space program, is an alien. David has 24 hours to prove it before Warren's nomination is confirmed, unaware that Warren is badly in need of regeneration.

David approaches James Baxter, a special investigator for the Senate sub-committee involved in the proceedings. David is able to arouse Baxter's doubts about Warren; but standing in the way of Baxter following up is his wife Celia. She's caught up in the fact that Warren is an impressive role model for their son and other members of their race; but her interference regarding Warren eventually jeopardizes David's life.

Cast

Roy Thinnes *(David Vincent)*
Raymond St. Jacques *(James Baxter)*
Janet MacLachlin *(Sarah Baxter)*
Roscoe Lee Browne *(Arnold Warren)*
Kent Smith *(Edgar Scoville)*
Louis Gossett, Jr. *(Ollie)*
Austin Willis *(William Gehrig)*
Joel Fluellen *(Homer Warren)*
Pepe Brown *(Michael Baxter)*
James Devine *(TV Stage Manager)*

#40. The Miracle

Produced by: Alan Armer
Teleplay by: Robert Collins
Story by: Robert Collins & Norman Herman
Directed by: Robert Day

Near a small New Mexico town is a tiny garden area with a statue of the Virgin Mary. According to legend, the Virgin appeared there to two Indian children and wept. Her tears formed the adjacent stream.

One afternoon, Beth Ferguson, a promiscuous teenager, sips water from beneath the holy statue and watches an alien die and incinerate. Before the incineration, the alien hands her a blue cloth bag containing a stone crystal and utters, "She will come for this." Beth believes that what she saw was a miracle. In reality, the crystal is needed to operate an alien laser weapon being brought to earth.

News of the miracle draws David to the small town. The crystal is displayed at Harry Ferguson's saloon where it lies in safekeeping for his daughter Beth. David offers to buy it from Harry, but an alien attempts to steal it, interrupting the sale. Harry manages to secure it in his safe, but now he wants more money. Beth is against selling it. She believes it to be a gift from God that has boosted her self-esteem and made her feel pure. Then, a beautiful but strange nun appears by the statue while Beth is deep in prayer. The nun asks for the stone crystal, thus reinforcing Beth's beliefs.

Cast

Roy Thinnes (*David Vincent*)
Barbara Hershey (*Beth Ferguson*)
Edward Asner (*Harry Ferguson*)
Arch Johnson (*Father Paul*)
Robert Biheller (*Ricky*)
Christopher Shea (*Johnny*)
Marion Thompson (*The Nun*)
Wayne Heffley (*Deputy*)
Rayford Barnes (*Alien Courier*)

#41. The Life Seekers

Produced by: Alan Armer
Written by: Laurence Heath
Directed by: Paul Wendkos

On a rural highway in Redstone, Indiana, Officer Joe Nash observes a speeding car and gives chase. After a brief pursuit, he pulls them over. When Nash sees a man in the back seat begin to glow, the driver shoots him. Nash returns fire and the driver incinerates. A woman passenger jumps into the driver's seat and the car speeds off.

News of the incident brings David to Redstone, but Nash is reluctant to discuss what happened, and his boss, Captain Battersea dismisses David as a crank.

Back at his motel, David receives a call from a woman pretending to have seen an alien. They arrange to meet. Beyond the charade, David meets Keith and his companion Claire, the two passengers in the car stopped by Nash. Keith and Claire are fugitive aliens marked for death by their compatriots because they favor the abandonment of earth as an objective (for moral and scientific reasons). Keith wants to return to his planet to show leadership a memory bank he carries containing a million facts about man, including his philosophy and science. He hopes this will change a great many minds about the planned invasion of earth. Millions of lives are at stake.

David agrees to help Keith and Claire through a police and alien dragnet to reach a planned rendezvous with a spacecraft that will take them back to their planet.

Cast

Roy Thinnes (*David Vincent*)
Barry Morse (*Keith*)
Diana Muldaur (*Claire*)
R. G. Armstrong (*Capt. Battersea*)
Kent Smith (Edgar Scoville)
Arthur Franz (Jim Trent)
Stephen Brooks (Officer Joe Nash)

Paul Comi (Sgt. Leeds)
Morgan Jones (Lt. Rawlings)
Herb Armstrong (Dr. Stark)
Barry Cahill (Dorsey)
Scott Graham (Donner)

#42. The Pursued

Produced by: Alan Armer
Written by: Don Brinkley
Directed by: William Hale

Anne Gibbs is an alien who is being used to experiment with human emotions, but things go awry and she develops dangerous and deadly mood swings. Now the invaders seek to destroy her so as not to call attention to themselves.

David is summoned by Anne to the Sycamore Guest House in a small Massachusetts town. However, she arrives before he does, pursued by two aliens. When co-owner Hattie Willis grows suspicious and attempts to call the sheriff, Anne loses control, kills her, and flees.

David eventually meets Anne in flight and Edgar Scoville arranges for a helicopter to take them to Washington, D.C. to meet with officials from the Justice Department. En route to the helicopter, David and Anne must elude the aliens and police, and David must deal with Anne's violent outbursts.

Cast

Roy Thinnes *(David Vincent)*
Suzanne Pleshette *(Anne Gibbs)*
Will Geer *(Hank Willis)*
Kent Smith *(Edgar Scoville)*
Richard O'Brien *(Charles McKay)*
Gene Lyons *(John Corwin)*
Mary Jackson *(Hattie Willis)*
Mike McGreevey *(Eddie McKay)*
Eldon Quick *(Antique Owner)*
Barry Williams *(Boy)*

#43. Inquisition

Produced by: Alan Armer
Written by: Barry Oringer
Directed by: Robert Glatzer

In Washington, D.C., David and Edgar Scoville brief Senator Robert Breeding that Arthur Coy, a technical advisor to the National Security Council may be an alien. Coy is a close friend of Breeding who is unreceptive to their claims.

After David and Edgar leave his office, a bomb explodes and kills Breeding. David and Edgar are taken to the office of Andrew Hatcher, special assistant to the Attorney General. Hatcher, a somewhat ruthless and ambitious prosecutor believes that David and Edgar are part of an underground organization that had the motive and opportunity to kill Breeding.

When the aliens manufacture evidence and a witness to support Hatcher's theory, a grand jury indictment leads to David and Edgar's arrest for murder. Meanwhile, Edgar's technicians uncover evidence that the aliens plan to end their reconnaissance and carry out an all-out assault.

Cast

Roy Thinnes *(David Vincent)*
Peter Mark Richman *(Andrew Hatcher)*
Susan Oliver *(Joan Seeley)*
John Milford *(Jim Boland)*
Kent Smith *(Edgar Scoville)*
Robert H. Harris *(Dr. Stan Frederickson)*
Stewart Moss *(Hadley Jenkins)*
Alex Gerry *(Senator Robert Breeding)*
Burt Douglas *(Alien)*
Mary Gregory *(Secretary)*
Lincoln Demyan *(Security)*
Ernest Harada *(Waiter)*
Michael Harris *(Policeman)*

THE END of Season Two

AUTHOR'S TOP TWENTY EPISODES
(in order of broadcast)

Episode	Title	Season
1	Beachhead	1
2	The Experiment	1
3	The Mutation	1
5	Genesis	1
7	Nightmare	1
10	The Innocent	1
11	The Ivy Curtain	1
13	Storm	1
14	Panic	1
16	Wall of Crystal	1
17	The Condemned	1
19	The Saucer	2
21	Valley of the Shadow	2
23	The Trial	2
25	Dark Outpost	2
29	Labyrinth	2
31	The Believers	2
41	The Life Seekers	2
42	The Pursued	2
43	Inquisition	2

NOTABLE PERFORMANCES

(in order of broadcast)

Roddy McDowell	*The Experiment*
Laurence Naismith	*The Experiment*
Suzanne Pleshette	*The Mutation*
Arthur Hill	*The Leeches*
John Larch	*Genesis*
Carol Rossen	*Genesis*
Jack Lord	*Vikor*
Kathleen Widdoes	*Nightmare*
James Whitmore	*Quantity Unknown*
Michael Rennie	*The Innocent*
Jack Warden	*The Ivy Curtain*
Joseph Campanella	*Storm*
Burgess Meredith	*Wall of Crystal*
Ralph Bellamy	*The Condemned*
Shirley Knight	*The Watchers*
Nan Martin	*Valley of the Shadow*
Dana Wynter	*The Captive*
Carol Lynley	*The Believers*
Laurence Naismith	*Ransom*
Karen Black	*Ransom*
Barbara Hershey	*The Miracle*
Barry Morse	*The Life Seekers*
Suzanne Pleshette	*The Pursued*

SERIES FACTS

DID YOU KNOW......

When Roy Thinnes first signed to play the role of David Vincent he was skeptical about UFO's. Then, three days before the series debut, Thinnes and his future wife actress Lynn Loring were witness to a UFO sighting. While driving west in Los Angeles' San Fernando Valley he described the following: "A UFO flew at an uncontrolled speed leaving a multi-colored track as it raced across the sky. After it disappeared beyond the horizon, it reappeared and flew back in the opposite direction changing colors as it went." Loring strongly suggested they report what they saw. Thinnes was reluctant. His show was about to premiere and he felt it would sound like a self-serving actor reporting a UFO given the subject matter of the series. However, within a short period of time there were radio reports of an unexplained sighting.

Series Director of Photography (DP) Andrew McIntyre was a bomber pilot during WWII. He related stories to Thinnes of entire formations of bomber planes being followed by disc-shaped objects during missions over Italy. As a result, McIntyre was a believer and years later he set the tone on the set. When an occasional director made off-hand comments about the series premise, McIntyre would take them aside and impress upon them that the crew took what they did very seriously.

Ironically, during a period where the network wanted to downplay the violence on television, *The Invaders* proved to be an exception. Stunt coordinator Glenn Wilder explained that it was because many of those killed on the series were alien beings bent on destroying the human race. When they were killed, they incinerated rapidly with no evidence of blood and gore. The network found that suitable for the younger audience watching the show.

In the original pilot, David Vincent struggles with an alien named John Brandon (played by James "Skip" Ward) in need of regeneration. Brandon begins to glow and his pupils turn black. Ward (or a stuntman in the shot) wore opaque contact lenses. That effect did not appear in the broadcast version and was never used during the run of the series.

The ABC Network never viewed the pilot in its entirety to give it a "green light." *The Invaders* was picked up as a midseason replacement midway through the filming of "Beachhead."

"Beachhead" the pilot episode was later remade as a segment of the 1977 Quinn Martin series *Tales of the Unexpected.* The episode was entitled "The Nomads." It featured actor David Birney as a Viet Nam veteran who discovers a colony of aliens who plan to take over the earth.

The budget for each episode was about $200,000.

David Vincent's travels would take him from Santa Barbara, California where he first saw the alien spaceship land to Pennsylvania, Texas, Rhode Island, Florida, Kansas, Utah, Maine, New Mexico, West Virginia, Oregon, Virginia, Wyoming, Indiana, Colorado, Vermont, Massachusetts, as well as abroad to a mountainous area ten miles from the Baltic Sea. In reality, he never traveled more than two to three hours from the Los Angeles area.

Roy Thinnes was 28 years old when he began filming the series. The character of David Vincent was 32.

DP Andrew McIntyre accentuated the blue eyes of Roy Thinnes by strategic placement of baby spots (lights). He felt it contributed to the supernatural aura of the series premise.

After his hair caught on fire during an action sequence in an early episode, stunt coordinator Glenn Wilder took extra precaution in future stunts involving flames. He would wear long underwear that was dipped in ice-cold water, covered by fire-retardent clothing that matched the wardrobe of series star Thinnes whom he was doubling. In addition, Wilder would make sure to douse his hair and face with water.

Because the invaders appeared in human form, Quinn Martin wanted their costumes to be simple. He rejected several samples before settling on dark green jump suits.

The first time the audience saw a regeneration chamber was in the pilot. The death disc first appeared in the second episode: "The Experiment." In the third segment: "The Mutation", the viewers first witnessed an alien communicator, their disintegrator canon, ray guns, and an alien immolation.

Most of the alien props were designed by veteran art director George Chan and made in-house in the mill at Goldwyn Studios. The control panels displayed in the alien space ship as well as other intricate-looking equipment was frequently made by companies who specialized in making dials, switches, lights and graphics. Other props were found at specialized Los Angeles area prop houses.

Some of the alien props were operated by special effects crew members. The cylinder portion of the Regeneration Chamber (manufactured by a plastics company) was raised and lowered by unseen cable wires. The Hypnotic Crystal device (composed of two artificial crystals) was spun by a monofilament wire (fine and lightweight) rendered mostly invisible on camera by dulling spray and lighting effect. (The glowing was achieved by lighting and an optical effect in the lab.)

The alien hand props such as the communicator, death disc and disintegrator gun were made from plastic or wood which was painted with a veneer to make it appear metallic on camera. The alien disintegrator gun used in the first season was deemed too big and bulky by the production staff. A smaller and more streamline version was used during season two. Both versions had the small viewfinder positioned on the top ramp toward the front of the gun.

Seven actors who played key roles in classic 1950s science fiction films appeared in The Invaders. Michael Rennie (Klatu in *The Day the Earth Stood Still)* was in "The Innocent" and "Summit Meeting" Parts 1 and 2; Peter Graves (Dr. Ed Wainwright in *Beginning of the End)* appeared in "Moonshot"; Kevin McCarthy, Dana Wynter and Virginia Christine (Dr. Miles Bennell, Becky Driscoll and Wilma Lentz in *Invasion of The Body Snatchers)* appeared in "The Watchers," "The Captive" and "Labyrinth" respectively; Anne Francis (Altaira in *Forbidden Planet)* was seen in "The Saucer" and Russell Johnson (George in *It Came from Outer Space)* appeared in "The Trial."

Seven actresses guest starred as aliens. They include Diane Baker ("Beachhead"), Suzanne Pleshette ("The Mutation," "The Pursued"), Nancy Wickwire ("The Betrayed"), Barbara Luna ("Storm"), Antionette Bower ("Condition Red"), Diana Hyland (Summit Meeting, Parts 1 and 2), and Diana Muldaur ("The Life Seekers.") Susan Pleshette was the only actress to portray two different aliens. Ironically, both characters had conflicted feelings, and were pursued by her fellow race out to destroy her. The only alien to have a romantic scene with David Vincent was Claire (Diana Muldaur). She was portrayed as the most peaceful and sympathetic among the group.

Alfred Ryder apparently played the same alien leader in three episodes: "Vikor," "Ransom," and "The Peacemaker." However, in "Vikor," he was billed as "Nexus," but "alien leader" in the later two segments.

Aliens were not exclusively played by adult actors. In "The Saucer", the youngest alien was played by nine year old Christopher Shea. In "The Pursued," thirteen year old Barry Williams (later on "The Brady Bunch") played an alien masquerading as a paperboy.

At the end of the 32nd episode "The Believers," it appeared that Elyse Reynolds (played by Carol Lynley) would join Edgar Scoville's group, lend her skills as a trained psychologist and reoccur in the final twelve episodes. She never did.

In the final thirteen segments, there was one episode, "The Miracle," where David Vincent appeared alone and was not aided by Edgar Scoville and his group of believers.

David Vincent who evaded death at the hands of the invaders, was finally killed in "The Ransom," the fifteenth episode of season two. During a fight with an alien, Vincent is electrocuted. However, the invaders are forced to bring him back to life by placing him in a regeneration chamber, to save the life of their leader.

On the final card of the first season screen credits, it stated the series was produced in association with the ABC Television Network. That credit was deleted from the end of the second season screen credits.

INVADER WEAPONS

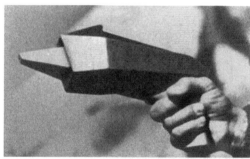

(Clockwise from above) The Death Disk—when applied to the back of a victim's neck it caused paralysis or a cerebral hemorrhage. The Ray Gun (first season model) sighted through a small screen on the top and incinerated the target. The insect caller/transmitter used in the episode "Nightmare." The hypnotic crystal device used to control its subject through mind control.

PRODUCTION STAFF

Executive Producer	Quinn Martin
Producer	Alan Armer
Associate Producer	Anthony Spinner (1967)
	David Rintels (1967–1968)
In Charge of Production	Arthur Fellows
	Adrian Samish
Assistant to the Producer	John Conwell
Production Managers	Fred Ahern
	Howard Alston
Post Production Supervisor	John Elizalde
Unit Production Managers	Robert Huddleston
	Robert G. Stone
Second Unit Director	Carl Barth
Assistant Directors	Robert Daley
	Lou Place
	Paul Wurtzel
	Donald C. Klune
	Harold Schneider
Cinematography	Andrew J. McIntyre
	Meredith Nicholson (Pilot)
Film Editors	Jerry Young
	Jodie Copelan
	Walter Hanneman
	Richard Cahoon
	Lee Gilbert
	Richard K. Brockway

Assistant Film Editors	Ray Daniels
	Martin Fox
	Tom Neff, Jr.
	Orven Schanzer
Second Cameraman	Gail Parker
Casting	Patricia Rose Mock
Art Directors	James D. Vance
	George B. Chan
Set Decorators	Sandy Grace
	Carl Biddiscombe
Key Grip	Larry Milton
Chief Electrician	Robert Farmer
Special Photographic Effects	Darrell A. Anderson
Special Effects	Ira Anderson
Stunts	Troy Melton
	Glenn Wilder
Costume Supervisor	Frank Beetson, Jr.
Property Master	Arthur Friedrich
	Ray Thompson
Production Mixer	Barry Thomas
Sound Editor	Eddie Campbell
	Werner Kirsch
Script Supervisor	Marshall Schlom
	John Dutton
Title Design	Wayne Fitzgerald
Series Music	Dominic Frontiere
	Duane Tatro
	Richard Markowitz
	Sidney Cutner
	Irving Gertz
Music Editor	Dan Carlin
Make-up	Jack Barron
Hair Stylist	Annabelle

BIOGRAPHIES

Alan A. Armer

At the age of fifteen, Alan Armer won the title of "World's Fastest Talker" in an NBC radio contest, reciting Lewis Carroll's *"The Walrus and the Carpenter"* (613 words) in 57 seconds. He's slowed down considerably since then.

After graduating from Stanford University with a B.A. in speech and drama, Armer tried his hand first in radio as a disc jockey for San Jose's KEEN and then in advertising, writing, staging, editing, narrating, even acting in early TV commercials. Because of what he learned about television, Armer was able to write and produce a weekly showcase for young professional actors, *Lights, Camera, Action* for Los Angeles station KNBH.

When the show expired three years later, Armer became a stage manager for the station. After six months he started directing and was a staff director there for over four years. When the days of live programming were fading, 20th Century Fox hired Armer to write and produce some of their early TV films.

During the next twenty years, Armer wrote, produced or directed over 350 television programs for Fox, Desilu, Quinn Martin Productions, Paramount, and Universal. Many of his series were in the top ten. They included *Broken Arrow, The Untouchables, The Fugitive, The Invaders, Name of the Game, Lancer,* and *Cannon,* plus a number of television movies.

During his years in television, Armer won almost every major industry award including the TV Academy's distinguished Emmy Award. Also: a Mystery Writers of America Award, TV Guide Award, Western Writers of America Award, and Sound

Editors Award. He served twice as president of the Hollywood Chapter of the Television Academy, and was a trustee to the National TV Academy.

After a successful career in television, Armer moved into academia. To enrich his teaching, he attended graduate school at UCLA and earned his M.A. degree. During his 20 years at California State University, Armer won a Distinguished Teaching Award and was honored, finally, to receive an honorary doctorate.

A year after retiring Armer was again honored when the university named its newest and most elegant auditorium the Armer Screening Room.

He has published two textbooks with Wadsworth Publishing Company: *Writing the Screenplay* and *Directing Television and Film.*

Diane Baker

Native Californian Diane Baker began her career as a contract player at 20th Century Fox. She made her film debut in *The Diary of Anne Frank* and shortly after she appeared in *Journey to the Center of the Earth*, and *The Best of Everything.*

Her notable career also includes producing several miniseries as well as episodes of the *CBS School Break Special* and *ABC After School Specials.*

Her many film credits include: *A Mighty Wind, On the Roof, Murder at 1600, Courage Under Fire, The Cable Guy, The Net, Imaginary Crimes, The Joy Luck Club, The Silence of the Lambs, The Closer, Baker's Hawk, Stigma, Krakatoa: East of Java, Mirage, Marnie, Strait-Jacket, The Prize, Nine Hours to Rama, The 300 Spartans*, and Hemingway's *Adventures of a Young Man.*

Television appearances include: *House M.D., Unscripted, Dragnet, First Monday, Law & Order: Special Victims Unit, Jackie Bouvier Kennedy Onassis, E.R., The Nanny, Astoria, Chicago Hope, Murder She Wrote, Perry Mason: The Case of the Heartbroken Bride, Civil Wars, The Haunted, A Woman of Substance, Fantasy*

Island, The Blue and the Gray, Trapper John M.D., The Love Boat, Kojak, Policy Story, Barnaby Jones, Marcus Welby M.D., The Streets of San Francisco, Lucas Tanner, Medical Center, Love American Style, Bonanza, Night Gallery, The Virginian, The Name of the Game, Mission Impossible, The Fugitive, Bob Hope Presents the Chrysler Theater, The Dangerous Days of Kiowa Jones, Hawk, Dr. Kildare, The Big Valley, Convoy, Inherit the Wind, Wagon Train, Mr. Novak, Route 66, The Nurses, Bus Stop, Adventures in Paradise, Follow the Sun, and *Playhouse 90.*

Ed Begley

Ed Begley was a veteran character actor in radio and on Broadway prior to his becoming a Tony and Academy Award winner. In television, he was a three-time Emmy nominee.

He first appeared in films during the late 1940s, and began to work in network TV in the early 1950s. His film work includes *Road to Salina, The Dunwich Horror, The Monitors, A Time to Sing, Hang 'em High, Wild in the Streets, Fire Creek, Billion Dollar Brain, The Violent Enemy, Warning Shot, Do Not Fold Spindle or Mutilate, The Oscar, The Unsinkable Molly Brown, Sweet Bird of Youth* (AA for Best Supporting Actor), *Odds Against Tomorrow, 12 Angry Men, Patterns, The Turning Point, Deadline U.S.A., On Dangerous Ground, Lone Star, Boots Malone, The Lady from Texas, You're in the Navy Now, Wyoming Mail, Dark City, Saddle Tramp, Convicted, Backfire, The Great Gatsby, It Happens Every Spring, Tulsa, Sorry Wrong Number, Deep Waters,* and *The Street with No Name.*

Television work includes *The Name of the Game, Hallmark Hall of Fame, The Silent Gun, The Ghost and Mrs. Muir, The Mod Squad, My Three Sons, The High Chaparral, Gunsmoke, The Wild Wild West, The Lucy Show, Bonanza, The Virginian, The F.B.I., Burke's Law, The Fugitive, Slattery's People, Dr. Kildare, The Dick Van Dyke Show, The Alfred Hitchcock Hour, Rawhide, Wagon Train, Ben Casey, Route 66, Going My Way, The Dick Powell Theatre, Naked City, The Defenders, Empire, Cain's Hundred, The New Breed, Target: The Corrupters,* and *The U.S. Steel Hour.*

Ralph Bellamy

Ralph Bellamy began an acting career in his late teens as a member of a traveling theater company. After years of stock and repertory, he made his Broadway debut in *Town Boy*. From the 1930s through the 1980s, Bellamy appeared in over 100 feature films.

He won critical acclaim for his portrayal of Franklin Delano Roosevelt in *Sunrise at Campobello*, both on stage and in the 1960 film.

With the advent of television, Bellamy starred in one of the earliest network TV series—*Man Against Crime* (1949). He later starred in *The Eleventh Hour* (1963–1964), *The Survivors* (1969), and *Most Deadly Game* (1970).

His many films include: *Pretty Woman, The Good Mother, Coming to America, Amazon Women on the Moon, Disorderlies, Trading Places, Cancel My Reservation, Rosemary's Baby, The Professionals, Sunrise at Campobello, The Court Martial of Billy Mitchell, Lady on a Train, Delightfully Dangerous, Guest in the House, Men of Texas, The Ghost of Frankenstein, The Wolf Man, Ellery Queen and the Murder Ring, Ellery Queen and the Perfect Crime, Dive Bomber, Affectionately Yours, Ellery Queen's Penthouse Mystery, Footsteps in the Dark, Ellery Queen-Master Detective, Brother Orchid, His Girl Friday, Coast Guard, Blind Alley, Trade Winds, Boy Meets Girl, Fools for Scandal, Counterfeit Lady, The Man Who Lived Twice, The Final Hour, Hands Across the Table, Navy Wife, Rendezvous at Midnight, Girl in Danger, One Is Guilty, Spitfire, Ever in My Heart, Rebecca of Sunnybrook Farm, Forbidden,* and *Surrender.*

Television appearances include: *Christine Cromwell, War and Remembrance, L.A. Law, Matlock, Hotel, The Twilight Zone, Space, Love Leads the Way: A True Story, The Winds of War, Little House on the Prairie, Fantasy Island, Aloha Paradise, Walking Tall, Power, The Millionaire, The Clone Master, Wheels, The Bob Newhart Show, Westside Medical, Hunter, Testimony of Two Men, Arthur Hailey's The Moneychangers, Once an Eagle, The Boy in the Plastic Bubble, McNaughton's Daughter, Return to Earth, Cannon,*

Medical Center, Search for the Gods, Adventures of the Queen, The Log of the Black Pearl, The Missiles of October, Owen Marshall: Counselor at Law, Something Evil, The Immortal, The F.B.I., The Virginian, CBS Playhouse, Gunsmoke, Run for Your Life, Wings of Fire, 12 O'Clock High, Bob Hope Presents the Chrysler Theatre, Rawhide, Dr. Kildare, Alcoa Premiere, Death Valley Days, Checkmate, Frontier Justice, The Barbara Stanwyck Show, The United States Steel Hour, Climax, Studio One, Schlitz Playhouse of Stars, Zane Grey Theater, The Ford Television Theatre, Playhouse 90, Goodyear Television Playhouse, General Electric Theater, and *Your Show of Shows.*

Larry Cohen

Larry Cohen grew up in Manhattan and graduated from the City College of New York. He began his writing career at age 21, scripting a segment of *Kraft Television Theatre*. Throughout the 1960s he wrote episodes of *The United States Steel Hour, Checkmate, Sam Benedict, Arrest and Trial* (the pilot), *Espionage, The Rat Patrol, The Nurses, The Fugitive,* and multiple stories and teleplays for the prestigious courtroom drama: *The Defenders* (for which he earned two awards from the Television Academy). He also created *Branded* (1964), *The Invaders* (1967), *Coronet Blue* (1967), and wrote and produced *The Blue Light* (1966).

From the 1970s on he would occasionally write for network television but Cohen opted to become an independent filmmaker who wrote, produced and directed many of his own screenplays. A critical analysis of his many films: *The Radical Allegories of an Independent Filmmaker* was published by McFarland Press.

His screenwriting credits include: *Messages Deleted, Connected, Captivity, Cellular* (story), *Phone Booth, Misbegotten, The Ex, Uncle Same, Invasion of Privacy, The Expert* (uncredited), *Guilty as Sin, Body Snatchers* (screen story), *Deadly Illusion, Best Seller, Scandalous* (story), *I the Jury, The American Success Company, El Condor, Daddy's Gone A-Hunting, Scream Baby Scream, I*

Deal in Danger, Return of the Seven, and *Blade Rider.*

His film work (as writer/producer/director) includes: *Wicked Stepmother, A Return to Salem's Lot, It's Alive III: Island of the Alive, The Stuff, Q, Full Moon High, It Lives Again, The Private Files of J. Edgar Hoover, God Told Me To, It's Alive, Hell Up in Harlem, Black Caesar*, and *Bone.*

(As writer/director): *The Ambulance, Deadly Illusion, Perfect Stranger* and *Special Effects.*

(As writer/producer): *Maniac Cop, Maniac Cop II, and Maniac Cop III: Badge of Silence.*

His TV credits include: Ed McBain's *87th Precinct: Heatwave, NYPD Blue, Desperado: Avalanche at Devil's Ridge, Sheriff Who?* (a pilot remade as the MOW The Evil Roy Slade), *Women of San Quentin* (story), *Man on the Outside, Griff, Columbo: An Exercise in Fatality* (story), *Shootout in a One-Dog Town* (story), *Columbo: Candidate for Crime* (story), *Columbo: An Old Port* (story), *Cool Million, In Broad Daylight, Kraft Suspense Theatre, Way Out*, and *Zane Grey Theater.*

Forest Compton

Forest Compton may be best remembered for his portrayal of District Attorney Mike Karr on *Edge of Night*, and as Colonel Edward Gray on *Gomer Pyle U.S.M.C.*

His many television appearances include *Ed, Neighbors, Goodbye Sadie, McBain, Rage of Angels: The Story Continues, The F.B.I., That Girl, Hogan's Heroes, Mannix, Mayberry R.F.D., My Three Sons, 12 O'Clock High, Arrest and Trial, The Fugitive, 77 Sunset Strip, The Twilight Zone, Hawaiian Eye, General Electric Theater, Checkmate, Route 66, The Roaring 20s, Hennessey, Fury, Black Saddle, Johnny Ringo*, and *Navy Log.*

James Daly

James Daly (the father of actress Tyne Daly and actor Tim Daly) began his television career in the 1950s when he appeared on series such as *Robert Montgomery Presents, Philco Television Playhouse, Suspense, The Web,* and *Danger.* He appeared in several hundred episodic TV shows from the 1950s through the 1970s, including his portrayal of Dr. Paul Lochner in the long-running CBS series *Medical Center* (1969–1976). His feature films include *The Resurrection of Zachary Wheeler, The Big Bounce, Planet of the Apes, Werner von Braun, The Young Stranger,* and *The Court Martial of Billy Mitchell.*

A sampling of his numerous TV credits include: *Roots: The Next Generation, The Storyteller, Ironside, The F.B.I., Star Trek, Judd for the Defense, Disneyland, The Virginian, CBS Playhouse, Hallmark Hall of Fame, Run for Your Life, Mission Impossible, Gunsmoke, Combat, Felony Squad, The Fugitive, Bob Hope Presents the Chrysler Theatre, The Road West, 12 O'Clock High, Dr. Kildare, The Nurses, Breaking Point, The Great Adventure, The Twilight Zone, The Ann Southern Show, Destiny West!, The Loretta Young Show, Suspicion, Alcoa Theatre, Studio One, The Ford Television Theatre, Goodyear Television Playhouse, Omnibus, The Alcoa Hour, Kraft Television Theatre, Front Row Center, The Millionaire, Climax,* and *Foreign Intrigue.*

Robert Day

Robert Day began his career as a camera operator in his native England on such English films as *1984, Storm Over the Nile, A Kid for Two Farthings, An Inspector Calls, The Man Between, The Red Beret, Flesh and Blood, Give Us This Day, Obsession, Silent Dust,* and *They Made Me a Fugitive.*

He began his Hollywood directorial career in the 1960s and subsequently directed feature films, many television movies, and episodic TV shows. His movie work includes *The Man with Bogart's Face, Tarzan and the Great River, Tarzan and the Val-*

ley of Gold, She, Tarzan's Three Challenges, Operation Snatch, The Rebel, Tarzan the Magnificent, Two Way Stretch, Bobbikins, Life in Emergency Ward 10, First Man into Space, The Highwayman, The Haunted Strangler, and *The Green Man.*

His many television movie credits include: *Fire: Trapped on the 37th Floor, Higher Ground, Celebration Family, The Quick and the Dead, The Lady from Yesterday, Hollywood Wives, Cook and Peary: The Race to the Pole, China Rose, Your Place…or Mine, Running Out, The Adventures of Pollyanne, Beyond Witch Mountain, Marian Rose White, Scruples, Peter and Paul, Walking Through the Fire, Murder by Natural Causes, The Initiation of Sarah, Black Market Baby, Giving Birth, Twin Detectives, A Home of Our Own, The Trial of Chaplain Jensen, Death Stalk, Of Men and Women, The Big Game, The Reluctant Heroes, Mr. and Mrs. Bo Jo Jones, In Broad Daylight,* and *Ritual of Evil.*

His episodic TV work includes *Disneyland, Dallas, Logan's Run, Kojak, Switch, Police Story, Kodiak, The Streets of San Francisco, Barnaby Jones, Ghost Story, Banyon, Cades County, The Bold Ones, Matt Lincoln, Ironside, Paris 7000, Lancer, The F.B.I., The Invaders, The Avengers, Rendezvous,* and *The Adventures of Robin Hood.*

Don Eitner

Don Eitner began his theatrical career in the mid-1950s, starring in the pilot film for the television series *West Point.* He went on to appear in more than 80 network television shows including *Dallas, Dynasty, Quincy M.E., Harry O., Owen Marshall: Counselor at Law, Mission Impossible, The F.B.I., The Invaders,* and *The Fugitive.*

In the mid-60s, he began teaching and directing at Los Angeles' Melrose Theater, where he staged 22 productions. Eitner subsequently founded and became the artistic director of American Theater Arts which produced more than 50 plays, and trained several hundred aspiring professional actors.

As a guest director at the Dallas Theater Center, Eitner

staged the critically acclaimed *Diary of a Madman* and *The Lion in Winter*, and would later return to Texas to become the General Manager and Artistic Director of the Corsicana Community Playhouse.

Upon his return to California, Eitner directed several productions at the Fullerton Civic Light Opera, and became the theatre arts instructor for the Southern California Music Theatre Association's summer program for youth.

In recent years, he has directed a revised version of *Diary of a Madman* and the award-winning one-woman production of Mariette Hartley's *If You Get to Bethlehem, You've Gone Too Far.*

Anne Francis

Beautiful as well as talented, Anne Francis began modeling as a child and by age 11 had graced the Broadway stage opposite Gertrude Lawrence in *Lady in the Dark*. She was later discovered by Daryl Zanuck and placed under contract to 20th Century Fox. Eventually Francis signed with M.G.M. and co-starred in several classic films of the 1950s. In the 1960s she guest-starred in many network television series and in 1965 she starred in the cult classic series *Honey West* for which she received an Emmy nomination, and won a Golden Globe Award.

Francis is also the author of a book entitled *"Voices from Home"* and has written, produced and directed an art film, *Gemini Rising* that has aired on PBS.

Her feature films include: *Funny Girl, More Dead Than Alive, The Love God, Brainstorm, The Satan Bug, The Crowded Sky, Girl of the Night, The Hired Gun, The Rack, Forbidden Planet, The Scarlet Coat, Blackboard Jungle, Battle Cry, Bad Day at Black Rock, Rogue Cop, Susan Slept Here, The Rocket Man, A Lion in the Streets, Dreamboat, Lydia Bailey, Elopement*, and *Summer Holiday.*

Her many television credits include: *Without a Trace, The Drew Carey Show, Nash Bridges, Home Improvement, Lover's Knot, Wings, Fortune Hunter, Dark Justice, Murder She Wrote, The Golden Girls, Matlock, Laguna Heat, Jack and the Fatman, Hard-*

castle and McCormick, Riptide, The Love Boat, Trapper John M.D., Simon & Simon, CHIPS, Fantasy Island, Dallas, Charlie's Angels, The Rebels, Quincy M.E., The Eddie Capra Mysteries, Hawaii Five-O, Police Woman, Ba Ba Black Sheep, Wonder Woman, Bert D'Angelo/Superstar, Mobile One, S.W.A.T., Petrocelli, Barnaby Jones, Ellery Queen, A Girl Named Sooner, Movin' On, Archer, Insight, Love American Style, The Virginian, Dan August, The Name of the Game, Mission Impossible, The Fugitive, The Alfred Hitchcock Hour, The Man from Uncle, Ben Casey, The Reporter, Death Valley Days, Temple Houston, Kraft Suspense Theater, Arrest and Trial, The Eleventh Hour, The Twilight Zone, Alcoa Premiere, The New Breed, Dr. Kildare, Route 66, Hong Kong, The Untouchables, Adventures in Paradise, Rawhide, Climax, and *Studio One.*

Don Gordon

After serving in the U.S. Navy during World War II (while still in his teens), Don Gordon decided to pursue an acting career. He first appeared as a hospital patient in the 20th Century Fox film *12 O'Clock High* (1949) and made his television debut on *Space Patrol* two years later.

His feature film work includes: *The Exorcist III, Skin Deep, Code Name: Vengeance, Lethal Weapon, The Beast Within, Omen III: The Final Conflict, The Towering Inferno, Papillon, The Mack, Slaughter, Fuzz, Edict, The Last Movie, WUSA, The Gamblers, Bullitt, Cry Tough, Revolt at Fort Laramie,* and *The Benny Goodman Story.*

His many network TV appearances include: *Diagnosis Murder, MacGyver, Remington Steele, Airwolf, Knight Rider, Simon & Simon, T.J. Hooker, The Love Boat, The Dukes of Hazzard, The Powers of Matthew Star, Matt Houston, Hart to Hart, Charlie's Angels, The Streets of San Francisco, The Bionic Woman, Cannon, Mannix, The Magician, The F.B.I., The Rookies, Banacek, The Name of the Game, The Wild Wild West, 12 O'Clock High, Voyage to the Bottom of the Sea, Peyton Place, Combat, The Fugitive, The Outer Limits, The Eleventh Hour, The Untouchables, The Defenders,*

The Deputy, Playhouse 90, Hawaiian Eye, Wanted: Dead or Alive, The Twilight Zone, Mr. Lucky, Alfred Hitchcock Presents, 77 Sunset Strip, Sugarfoot, and *Trackdown.*

Peter Graves

The younger brother of James Arness, Peter Graves grew up in Minnesota. While still in his teens, he worked as a radio announcer. Following a two-year stint in the Air Force, Graves studied drama at the University of Minnesota and shortly after went to Hollywood.

He is best remembered for his portrayal of Jim Newton in the 1950s TV series *Fury,* and as Jim Phelps in *Mission Impossible* (1967–1973); (1988–1990). He was also the host of *Biography* (1994–2006).

His film work includes *Number One with a Bullet, Airplane: The Sequel, Savannah Smiles, Airplane, The Ballad of Josie, Texas Across the River, A Rage to Live, A Stranger in My Arms, Wolf Larsen, Beginning of the End, Canyon River, The Court Martial of Billy Mitchell, Fort Yuma, The Naked Street, The Night of the Hunter, Wichita, Robbers' Roost, The Long Gray Line, Black Tuesday, The Raid, The Yellow Tomahawk, Killers from Space, Beneath the 12-Mile Reef, East of Sumatra, War Paint, Stalag 17, Red Planet Mars, Angels in the Outfield, Fort Defiance,* and *Rogue River.*

His many TV credits include: *American Dad, 7th Heaven* (as John "The Colonel" Camden), *Cold Case, House M.D., With You in Spirit, Diagnosis Murder, The Angry Beaver, Burke's Law, The Golden Girls, War and Remembrance, Life with Lucy, Murder She Wrote, Fantasy Island, The Winds of War, Simon & Simon, Best of Friends, The Love Boat, Buck Rodgers in the 25th Century, Death Car on the Freeway, The Rebels, Disneyland, The Gift of the Magi, SST Death Flight, Where Have All the People Gone?, Underground Man, The President's Plane Is Missing, Call to Danger, The F.B.I., 12 O'Clock High, Daniel Boone, Run for Your Life, Branded, Laredo, The Great Adventure, The Virginian, The Farmer's Daughter, Kraft Suspense Theatre, The Alfred Hitchcock Hour, Route 66, Whiplash,*

Cimarron City, Climax, The Millionaire, Studio One, Fireside Theatre, TV Reader's Digest, and *Schlitz Playhouse of Stars.*

Gene Hackman

After training at the Pasadena Playhouse, Gene Hackman acted in summer stock and off-Broadway. He made his Broadway debut in *Any Wednesday* (1964) and that same year his film debut in *Lilith* (which starred Warren Beatty and Jean Seberg).

Hackman was nominated for Best Supporting Actor for his role in *Bonnie and Clyde* (1967), and for Best Actor in *I Never Sang for My Father* (1970). He won the Oscar for his portrayal of Detective "Popeye" Doyle in *The French Connection* (1972). He later won another Oscar for his work in *Unforgiven* (1992).

His prolific film career includes: *Welcome to Mooseport, Runaway Jury, Behind Enemy Lines, The Royal Tenenbaums, Heist, Heartbreakers, The Mexican, The Replacements, Under Suspicion, Enemy of the State, Twilight, Absolute Power, The Chamber, Extreme Measures, The Birdcage, Get Shorty, Crimson Tide, The Quick and the Dead, Wyatt Earp, Geronimo: An American Legend, The Firm, Company Business, Class Action, Narrow Margin, Postcards from the Edge, Loose Cannons, The Package, Mississippi Burning, Full Moon in Blue Water, Split Decisions, Another Woman, Bat 21, No Way Out, Superman IV: The Quest for Peace, Hoosiers, Power Target, Twice in a Lifetime, Misunderstood, Uncommon Valor, Two of a Kind, Under Fire, Eureka, Reds, All Night Long, Superman II, Superman, March or Die, A Bridge Too Far, The Domino Principle, Lucky Lady, Bite the Bullet, Night Moves, French Connection II, Young Frankenstein, Zandy's Bride, The Conversation, Scarecrow, The Poseidon Adventure, Prime Cut, Cisco Pike, The French Connection, The Hunting Party, Doctors' Wives, Marooned, Downhill Racer, The Gypsy Moths, Riot, The Split, A Covenant with Death, First to Fight,* and *Hawaii.*

His TV appearances include: *Insight, Shadow on the Lane, I Spy, The Iron Horse, CBS Playhouse, The F.B.I., Hawk, The Trials of O'Brien, Brenner, East Side West Side, Route 66, The Defenders, Naked City,* and *The United States Steel Hour.*

William Hale (a/k/a Billy Hale)

A prolific director from the mid-1960s through the 1980s, Billy Hale was originally a second unit director on George Steven's *The Greatest Story Ever Told.* His films include *Deadly Roulette, Gunfight in Abilene,* and *Journey to Shiloh.*

For many years Hale enjoyed an ongoing association with the Quinn Martin organization, directing episodes of *The F.B.I., The Invaders, Cannon, Barnaby Jones, The Streets of San Francisco, Bert D'Angelo/Superstar,* and *Caribe.* His additional television directorial credits (both long form and episodic) include: *People Like Us, Liberace, Lace II, Lace, The Denim Murder Case, One Show Makes It Murder, S.O.S. Titanic, The Paper Chase, Red Alert, The Killer Who Wouldn't Die, Crossfire, The Great Niagara, Kojak, Night Gallery, The Interns, Lancer, Judd for the Defense, Felony Squad, Bob Hope Presents the Chrysler Theater, Run for Your Life, How I Spent My Summer Vacation, The Time Tunnel, The Fugitive,* and *The Virginian.*

Barbara Hershey

Barbara Hershey began her career as a teenage actress in the mid-1960s appearing on such TV shows as *The Farmer's Daughter, Gidget,* and *Bob Hope Presents the Chrysler Theatre.* From 1966–1967 she co-starred as Kathy Monroe in the ABC television series *The Monroes* about a pioneer family in the old West. Soon after, Hershey began to appear in feature films and over the next four decades she has continued to play a wide range of roles in both movies and television.

Her film work includes: *Albert Schweitzer, Childless, Uncross the Stars, Love Comes Lately, The Bird Can't Fly, Riding the Bullet, Lantana, Passion, Breakfast of Champions, Drowning on Dry*

Land, The Portrait of a Lady, The Pallbearer, Last of the Dogmen, A Dangerous Woman, Swing Kids, Splitting Heirs, Falling Down, The Public Eye, Defenseless, Paris Trout, Tune in Tomorrow, Beaches, The Last Temptation of Christ, A World Apart, Shy People, Tin Men, Hoosiers, Hannah and Her Sisters, The Natural, Americana, The Right Stuff, The Entity, The Stunt Man, The Last Hard Men, Diamonds, You and Me, Boxcar Bertha, The Pursuit of Happiness, The Baby Maker, The Liberation of L.B. Jones, Last Summer, Heaven with a Gun, and *With Six You Get Eggroll.*

Her television appearances include: *Anne of Green Gables, The Mountain* (as Gennie Carver), *Paradise, The Stranger Beside Me, Hunger Point, Chicago Hope* (as Dr. Francesca Alberghetti), *The Staircase, Abraham, Return to Lonesome Dove, A Killing in a Small Town, Passion Flower, Alfred Hitchcock Presents, My Wicked Wicked Ways: The Legend of Errol Flynn, From Here to Eternity* (as Karen Holmes), *A Man Called Intrepid, Sunshine Christmas, In the Glitter Palace, Flood!, Kung Fu, Love Story, Insight, The High Chaparral, Run for Your Life*, and *Daniel Boone.*

Shirley Knight

Emmy and Tony Award winner Shirley Knight was also twice nominated for an Oscar for her performance in *Sweet Bird of Youth* and *The Dark at the Top of the Stairs.* Her films include *Listen to Your Heart, Paul Blart: Mall Cop, The Other Side of the Tracks, Open Window, To Lie in Green Pastures, A House on a Hill, Divine Secrets of the Ya-Ya Sisterhood, P.S. Your Cat is Dead, The Salton Sea, Angel Eyes, The Fugitive, 75 Degrees in July, As Good as it Gets, Little Boy Blue, Diabolique, Death in Venice, Color of Night, Endless Love, Beyond the Poseidon Adventure, Juggernaut, Secrets, The Rain People, Petulia, The Counterfeit Killer, The Group, Flight From Ayisha*, and *Ice Palace.*

Television credits: *Desperate Housewives, The Unit, House M.D., Cold Case, Crossing Jordan, Sudbury, Law & Order: Special Victim's Unit, E.R., Ally McBeal, Chicken Soup for the Soul, Maggie*

*Winters, A Marriage of Convenience, A Father for Brittany,
Significant Others, The Uninvited, Cybill, Children of the Dust,
N.Y.P.D. Blue, Dad, Angel and Me, The Yarn Princess, Baby Brokers,
The Secret Life of Houses, A Mother's Revenge, Angel Falls, L.A.
Law, Law & Order, Matlock, Thirty Something, Murder She Wrote,
The Equalizer, Billionaire Boys Club, Spenser: For Hire, Nurse,
Playing for Time, Champions: A Love Story, The Defection of Simas
Kudirka, 21 Hours at Munich, Return to Earth, Barnaby Jones, The
Manhunter, Nakia, Marcus Welby M.D., Medical Center, The Streets
of San Francisco, Alias Smith and Jones, The Bold Ones, The Fugitive,
The Virginian, The Defenders, The Outer Limits, Arrest and Trial,
The Eleventh Hour,* and *Naked City.*

Jack Lord

Jack Lord is best remembered for his portrayal of Steve
McGarrett on the long-running CBS television series *Hawaii
Five-O* (1968–1980) and his earlier series Stoney Burke (1962–
1963). He also owns the distinction of engaging in one of the
longest fight scenes ever recorded on film (with Gary Cooper)
in *Man of the West* (1958). In addition to a successful acting
career, Lord was also an accomplished artist.

His film credits include: *The Counterfeit Killer, Ride to
Hangman's Tree, Dr. No, Walk Like a Dragon, The Hangman, God's
Little Acre, The True Story of Lynn Stuart, Tip on a Dead Jockey,
Williamsburg: The Story of a Patriot, The Vagabond King, The
Court Marshall of Billy Mitchell, Cry Murder,* and *Project X.*

His television appearances include: *The High Chaparral,
The Doomsday Flight, The Man from Uncle, Ironside, The Fugitive,
Bob Hope Presents the Chrysler Theater, The Virginian, The F.B.I., 12
O'Clock High, Laredo, Combat, The Loner, Kraft Suspense Theatre,
Wagon Train, The Reporter, The Greatest Show on Earth, Dr.
Kildare, Checkmate, Cain's Hundred, Rawhide, Stagecoach West,
Outlaws, Route 66, Naked City, Bonanza, One Step Beyond, The
Lineup, The Untouchables, The Loretta Young Show, The Millionaire,*

U.S. Marshall, Playhouse 90, Gunsmoke, Have Gun-Will Travel, Climax!, Studio One, Armstrong Circle Theatre, Danger, Suspense, and *Man Against Crime.*

Lynn Loring

Lynn Loring began as a child actress on the CBS daytime drama *Search for Tomorrow* in the early 1950s. Throughout the 1960s and well into the 1970s, she guest-starred on numerous network television series. From 1965–1966 she co-starred on *The F.B.I.* as Barbara Erskine. She also appeared as Betty Anderson on the daytime serial *Return to Peyton Place* in the early 1970s.

Loring later moved into producing. As a producer, her films include *Me and the Kid,* and *Mr. Mom.* Her television movies include: *Making of a Male Model, Sizzle, The Best Little Girl in the World,* and *Return of the Mod Squad.*

Her television credits (as an actress) include: *The Kansas City Massacre, The Desperate Miles, Police Woman, The Horror at 37,000 Feet, Ghost Story, The Mod Squad, Black Noon, The Young Lawyers, The Immortal, Lancer, My Three Sons, The Man from Uncle, Bob Hope Presents the Chrysler Theatre, Bonanza, Baby Makes Three, A Man Called Shenandoah, The Wild Wild West, Burke's Law, The Big Valley, The Alfred Hitchcock Hour, Mr. Novak, Daniel Boone, Perry Mason, The Greatest Show on Earth, The Defenders, Gunsmoke, The Eleventh Hour, Fair Exchange, The Many Loves of Dobie Gillis, Target: The Corruptors, Wagon Train, Bus Stop, Armstrong Circle Theatre, Robert Montgomery Presents, Hallmark Hall of Fame,* and *Studio One.*

Her film appearances include: *Journey to the Far Side of the Sun, Pressure Point,* and *Splendor in the Grass.*

Tom Lowell

Originally from suburban Philadelphia, Tom Lowell began appearing in network television series in the early 1960s. He portrayed Billy Nelson on *Combat* for two seasons (1962–1964). He also appeared in feature films such as *Mr. Hobbs Takes a Vacation*, *The Manchurian Candidate*, *The Carpetbaggers*, *That Darn Cat*, *The Gnome-Mobile*, *The Boatniks*, and *Escape from the Planet of the Apes*.

His television work includes *Days of Our Lives*, *Quincy M.E.*, *The F.B.I.*, *Love American Style*, *Green Acres*, *Family Affair*, *Death Valley Days*, *Gomer Pyle U.S.M.C.*, *Daniel Boone*, *The Big Valley*, *Felony Squad*, *The Long Hot Summer*, *Bonanza*, *The Loner*, *Disneyland*, *The Addams Family*, *Gunsmoke*, *Perry Mason*, *Mr. Novak*, *The Alfred Hitchcock Hour*, *It's a Man's World*, and *The Twilight Zone*.

Barbara Luna

Born in Manhattan, Barbara Luna virtualy grew up on Broadway. She first appeared as Ngana in *South Pacific* (speaking her role entirely in French), followed by her appearance in *The King and I* (as one of the Siamese children.) While still in her teens, she landed the starring role in the first national tour of *Teahouse of the August Moon*. While touring, Luna was discovered by producer/director Mervyn Leroy and cast as Camille, the blind love interest of Frank Sinatra in *The Devil at 4 O'Clock* (co-starring Spencer Tracy). This led to other film roles in Stanley Kramer's *Ship of Fools* with Vivien Leigh and Lee Marvin; and *Firecreek* with James Stewart and Henry Fonda.

In addition to her continued movie roles, Luna guest-starred in nearly 500 television shows such as *Walt Disney's Zorro*, *Adventures in Paradise*, *The Outer Limits*, *Burke's Law*, *The Wild Wild West*, *Star Trek* (in the classic *"Mirror, Mirror"* episode), *The Man from U.N.C.L.E.*, *The Big Valley*, *The High Chaparral*, *The F.B.I.*, *Mission Impossible*, *Marcus Welby M.D.*, *Mannix*, *Char-*

lie's Angels, Buck Rogers in the 25th Century, Fantasy Island, Search for Tomorrow, One Life to Live, The Cosby Show, Dallas, Sunset Beach and Star Trek: New Voyages.

In between film and TV roles, Luna has returned to Broadway as Anita in a revival of West Side Story, and as Diana Morales in A Chorus Line.

Carol Lynley

Carol Lynley was originally a popular teenage model who graced the cover of Life Magazine. She made her film debut for Walt Disney in The Light in the Forest at the age of 15. Her subsequent film work includes Holiday for Lovers, Blue Denim, Hound-Dog Man, Return to Peyton Place, The Last Sunset, The Stripper, Under the Yum Yum Tree, The Cardinal, Shock Treatment, The Pleasure Seekers, Harlow, Bunny Lake is Missing, The Shuttered Room, The Maltese Bippy, Once You Kiss a Stranger, Norwood, The Poseidon Adventure, Cotter, The Four Deuces, The Washington Affair, The Cat and the Canary, The Shape of Things to Come, Dark Tower, Blackout, Spirits, Neon Signs, Drowning on Dry Land, and Vic.

Her many television guess appearances include: Night Heat, Finder of Lost Loves, Tales of the Unexpected, Fantasy Island, Hotel, The Fall Guy, Hart to Hart, Best of Friends, Charlie's Angels, The Littlest Hobo, The Love Boat, Sword of Justice, Hawaii Five-O, Kojak, Police Woman, Quincy M.E., Thriller, The Magician, The Sixth Sense, Night Gallery, Mannix, The Night Stalker, Weekend of Terror, The Most Deadly Game, The Bold Ones, The Immortal, It Takes a Thief, The Big Valley, The F.B.I., Run for Your Life, The Dick Powell Theater, The Virginian, Alcoa Premiere, and The Alfred Hitchcock Hour.

Quinn Martin

Quinn Martin was one of the most prolific and successful television producers of all time. He was born in New York and moved to California as a youngster when his father became a film editor. Martin also first worked as a film editor, then worked in a variety of behind-the-camera jobs before turning to writing and producing.

While working at Desilu, he produced a two-part episode of *The Untouchables* (for *Desilu Playhouse*) in 1959, which he turned into a series and produced the first season. In 1961 he created his own company: Q.M. Productions. Throughout the next two decades, Martin produced 16 one-hour series and 20 television movies. Q.M. Productions was sold to Taft Broadcasting Company in 1979. Martin later became an adjunct professor at the University of California.

His television series include *The New Breed* (1961–1962), *The Fugitive* (1963–1967), *Twelve O'Clock High* (1964–1967), *The F.B.I.* (1965–1974), *The Invaders* (1967–1968), *Cannon* (1971–1976), *The Streets of San Francisco* (1972–1977), *Banyon* (1972–1973), *Barnaby Jones* (1973–1980), *Manhunter* (1974–1975), *Caribe* (1975), *Bert D'Angelo/Superstar* (1976), *Most Wanted* (1976–1977), *Tales of the Unexpected* (1977), and *The Runaways* (1978–1979).

Kevin McCarthy

Kevin McCarthy's career spans seven decades. Originally a stage-trained actor who frequently appeared on Broadway, McCarthy has also appeared in countless feature films including his memorable performance as Dr. Miles Bennell in the sci-fi classic *Invasion of the Body Snatchers*. His numerous film credits include: *Fallen Angels, The Legend of Razorback, Just Causes, Judicial Consent, The Distinguished Gentleman, Final Approach, Innerspace, Dark Tower, Twilight Zone: The Movie, The Howling, Those Lips, Those Eyes, Hero at Large, Piranha, Kansas City Bomber, The Hell with Heroes, Hotel, A Big Hand for the Little Lady, Mirage, The Best Man, The Prize, A Gathering of Eagles, 40 Pounds of Trouble, The Misfits, An Annapolis Story, The Gambler from Natchez,* and *Death of a Salesman.*

His many TV appearances include: *The District, Early Edition, Boston Common, The Sister-in-Law, Murder She Wrote, Father Dowling Mysteries, Matlock, China Beach, Simon & Simon, In the Heat of the Night, Head of the Class, The Long Journey Home, The Colbys, Poor Little Rich Girl: The Barbara Hutton Story, LBJ: The Early Years, Fame, The Golden Girls, The A-Team, Scarecrow and Mrs. King, Dynasty, Fantasy Island, The Love Boat, Flamingo Road, The Oregon Trail, Hawaii Five-O, Cannon, Banacek, Mission Impossible, Julia, The Survivors* (as Philip Hastings), *The F.B.I., The Guns of Will Sonnett, The High Chaparral, The Name of the Game, Judd for the Defense, Felony Squad, The Road West, 12 O'Clock High, The Man from Uncle, Burke's Law, The Fugitive, Dr. Kildare, Alfred Hitchcock Presents, The Eleventh Hour, Breaking Point, The Defenders, The Rifleman, Going My Way,* and *Ben Casey.*

Burgess Meredith

Burgess Meredith began his acting career as a member of Eva Le Gallienne's theater group in New York's early 1930s. He made his film debut in *Winterset* (1936). Over the years he appeared in a variety of film and television roles, and is best remembered as the Penguin in *Batman,* and as Mickey Goldmill in the *Rocky* films.

His many films include *Grumpier Old Men, Across the Moon, Grumpy Old Men, State of Grace, Full Moon in Blue Water, Santa Claus, True Confessions, Clash of the Titans, The Last Chase, Final Assignment, When Time Ran Out, The Great Bank Hoax, Magic, Foul Play, The Manitou, The Sentinel, Burnt Offerings, The Hindenburg, The Master Gunfighter, 92 in the Shade, The Day of the Locust, The Man, Such Good Friends, There Was a Crooked Man, Mackenna's Gold, Hurry Sundown, Batman: The Movie, In Harm's Way, The Cardinal, Advise and Consent, Story of G.I. Joe,*

That Uncertain Feeling, Castle on the Hudson, Of Mice and Men, Idiot's Delight, and *Winterset.*

Television credits include: *In the Heat of the Night, Outrage, Gloria, Archie Bunker's Place, The Return of Captain Nemo, SST: Death Flight, Tail Gunner Joe, Old Faithful, Night Gallery, Probe, McCloud, Ironside, Love American Style, Lock Stock and Barrel, The Name of the Game, The Bold Ones, Daniel Boone, Bonanza, Branded, Please Don't Eat the Daisies, 12 O'Clock High, The Loner, Trials of O'Brien, The Wild Wild West, Laredo, Mr. Novak, Burke's Law, Rawhide, Wagon Train, The Travels of Jamie McPheeters, Breaking Point,* 77 *Sunset Strip, The Twilight Zone, Ben Casey, Sam Benedict, The Eleventh Hour, Naked City, General Electric Theater, The United States Steel Hour, Tales of Tomorrow, Philco Television Playhouse, Studio One, Robert Montgomery Presents,* and *Your Show of Shows.*

Barry Morse

Barry Morse began his career on stage in his native England and he later worked in Canadian theater and radio. He is best remembered as the relentless Lt. Gerard in pursuit of Richard Kimble (David Janssen) in *The Fugitive* (1963–1967). He later co-starred opposite Martin Landau and Barbara Bain in *Space 1999.*

His film appearances include *Taxman, The Changeling, Klondike Fever, The Shape of Things to Come, Power Play, One Man, Asylum, Running Scared,* and *Puzzle of a Downfall Child.*

His many television credits include: *Icon, Doctors, Waking the Dead, Anne of Green Gables: The Continuing Story, La Femme Nikita, Space Island One, Sirens, JFK: Reckless Youth, Dracula: The Series, War and Remembrance, The Twilight Zone, The Return of Sherlock Holmes, Covenant, Reunion at Fairborough, A Woman of Substance, Master of the Game, Sadat, The Winds of War, The Rothko Conspiracy, The Story of David, The Adventurer, N.Y.P.D., The F.B.I., Judd for the Defense, The Saint, Profiles in Courage, The Nurses, Naked City, Alcoa Premiere, Adventures in Paradise, Suspense,* and *Playhouse 90.*

Susan Oliver

Born in New York City, Susan Oliver trained at the Neighborhood Playhouse, and first appeared in live television dramas in the mid-1950s. She made her Broadway debut in 1958, and won a Tony Award for "best newcomer." Soon after, she went to Hollywood and appeared in countless television shows over the next three decades. In the early 1980s she directed episodes of *MASH* and *Trapper John, M.D.*

Oliver was also a licensed pilot and attempted to become the first woman to fly a single-engine plane from New York to Moscow.

Her network TV appearances include: *Freddy's Nightmares, Simon & Simon, Murder She Wrote, International Airport, Magnum P.I., Tomorrow's Child, The Love Boat, The Streets of San Francisco, Amelia Earhart, Days of Our Lives, The Manhunter, Police Story, Petrocelli, Barnaby Jones, Love Story, The Magician, The F.B.I., Ghost Story, Cannon, Gunsmoke, Medical Center, The Smith Family, Night Gallery, Sarge, Longstreet, The D.A., Love American Style, Alias Smith and Jones, Dan August, The Name of the Game, The Virginian, Mannix, The Big Valley, The Outsider, A Man Called Gannon, The Wild Wild West, T·H·E· Cat, Tarzan, My Three Sons, Star Trek, Peyton Place* (as Ann Howard), *I Spy, Gomer Pyle U.S.M.C., A Man Called Shenandoah, Dr. Kildare, The Man From Uncle, Ben Casey, The Rogues, Destry, The Defenders, The Travels of Jamie McPheeters, The Andy Griffith Show, Burke's Law, The Fugitive, The Nurses, 77 Sunset Strip, Route 66, The Dick Powell Show, Wagon Train, Rawhide, The Alfred Hitchcock Hour, Checkmate, Cain's Hundred, Laramie, The Adventures of Ozzie and Harriet, Adventures in Paradise, Zane Grey Theater, Naked City, Michael Shayne, The Aquanauts, The Untouchables, Thriller, Wanted Dead or Alive, The Twilight Zone, Playhouse 90, Bonanza, The Lineup, The Millionaire, Father Knows Best, Climax, The United States Steel Hour;* and *Studio One.*

Her film credits include *Hardly Working, Ginger in the Morning, The Monitors, Change of Mind, The Love-Ins, The*

Disorderly Orderly, Your Cheatin' Heart, Looking for Love, Guns of Diablo, The Caretakers, Butterfield 8, and *The Gene Krupa Story.*

Suzanne Pleshette

The proud possessor of beauty, talent, and a unique personality, Suzanne Pleshette enjoyed a lengthy career in films and television. She made her Broadway debut in *Compulsion* and later replaced Ann Bancroft in *The Miracle Worker.* She first appeared on television in the TV series *Harbourmaster* in 1957.

Her films include: *Oh God Book II, Hot Stuff, The Shaggy D.A., Support Your Local Gunfighter, Suppose They Gave a War and Nobody Came?, If It's Tuesday This Must Be Belgium, Target: Harry, The Power, Blackbeard's Ghost, The Adventures of Bullwhip Griffin, Mister Buddwing, Nevada Smith, The Ugly Dachshund, A Rage to Live, Youngblood Hawke, Fate Is the Hunter, A Distant Trumpet, Wall of Noise, The Birds, 40 Pounds of Trouble, Rome Adventure,* and *The Geisha Boy.*

Her many television appearances include *Will & Grace, 8 Simple Rules… for Dating My Teenage Daughter, Good Morning Miami, The Boys Are Back, A Twist of the Knife, Battling for Baby, The Bob Newhart Show 19th Anniversary Special, Leona Helmsley: The Queen of Mean, Nightingales, Alone in the Neon Jungle, A Stranger Waits, Bridges to Cross, Kojak: The Belarus File, Suzanne Pleshette is Maggie Briggs, One Cooks the Other Doesn't, Dixie: Changing Habits, Fantasies, Help Wanted: Male, The Star Maker, If Things Were Different, Flesh & Blood, Kate Bliss and the Ticker Tape Kid, The Bob Newhart Show* (as Emily Hartley), *Richie Brockelman: The Missing 24 Hours, Law and Order, The Legend of Valentino, Bonanza, Ironside, Medical Center, Columbo, In Broad Daylight, River of Gold, The Name of the Game, The F.B.I., The Courtship of Eddie's Father, Marcus Welby M.D., Gunsmoke, Love American Style, Hunters Are for Killing, Along Came a Spider, It Takes a Thief, Cimarron Strip, Bob Hope Presents the Chrysler Theater, The Fugitive, The Wild Wild West, Dr. Kildare, Channing,*

Wagon Train, Alcoa Premiere, The Dick Powell Show, Ben Casey, Route 66, General Electric Theater, Target: The Corruptors, The Tab Hunter Show, Hong Kong, The Islanders, Naked City, Riverboat, Alfred Hitchcock Presents, Adventures in Paradise, Black Saddle, Playhouse 90, One Step Beyond, The Third Man, Have Gun-Will Travel, and *Decoy.*

Michael Rennie

Englishman Michael Rennie began his career doing repertory theater in several British provinces, then appeared in English films of the 1940s. In 1951 he was brought to the U.S. and placed under contract to 20th Century Fox as the star of the sci-fi classic *The Day the Earth Stood Still.* He appeared in numerous films throughout the decade. From 1959–1965 he starred as Harry Lime in the British TV series *The Third Man.*

Feature film work: *The Battle of El Alamein, The Gold Seekers, The Devil's Brigade, The Power, Hotel, Death on the Run, Ride Beyond Vengeance, Cyborg 2087, Mary Mary, Omar Khayyam, Island in the Sun, Teenage Rebel, The Rains of Ranchipur, Seven Cities of Gold, Soldier of Fortune, Desirée, Mambo, Demetrius and the Gladiators, Princess of the Nile, King of the Khyber Rifles, The Robe, Dangerous Crossing, Single-Handed, Les Miserables, Five Fingers, Phone Call from a Stranger, The House in the Square, The 13th Letter,* and *The Black Robe.*

Network television: *The F.B.I., The Danny Thomas Hour, The Man from Under, I Spy, Hondo, The Iron Horse, Bob Hope Presents the Chrysler Theater, Batman, Jericho, Daniel Boone, The Time Tunnel, Lost in Space, 12 O'Clock High, Branded, Kraft Suspense Theatre, Bonanza, The Great Adventure, Wagon Train, The Alfred Hitchcock Hour, The Virginian, Perry Mason, The Dick Powell Theatre, Route 66, The Barbara Stanwyck Show, Zane Grey Theater, Suspicion,* and *Climax.*

Peter Mark Richman

Peter Mark Richman draws from a deep well of experience on the Broadway stage, motion pictures and television. He debuted on Broadway as Johnny Pope in *A Hatful of Rain* and toured nationally with Vivian Blaine. Following, he appeared in *Masquerade* opposite Cloris Leachman, and portrayed Jerry in over 400 performances of Edward Albee's original New York production of *The Zoo Story*.

William Wyler brought him west for the classic film *Friendly Pesuasion* with Gary Cooper and Dorothy McGuire. Other films include *The Black Orchid* with Sophia Loren and Anthony Quinn, *The Strange One, The Dark Intruder, Judgment Day* and *Pool Hall Junkies*. He also starred in the films *Friday the 13th, Part 8*, and *Naked Gun 2 1/2*.

On television Richman starred as Nick Cain in the NBC series *Cain's Hundred*, and made over 500 guest star appearances on such shows as *The Virginian, Twilight Zone, The F.B.I., Mission Impossible, Murder She Wrote, Fantasy Island, Star Trek: The Next Generation*, and *Beverly Hills 90210*. He co-starred on the ABC series *Longstreet*, recurred as Rev. Snow on *Three's Company*, and as attorney Andrew Laird on *Dynasty* for four seasons. He also created the role of C.C. Capwell on the daytime drama *Santa Barbara*.

An accomplished painter, he has had 17 critically acclaimed one-man exhibitions. As a writer, ANTA and the Actors Studio have produced his one-act plays. His full length play *Medal for Murray* recently received a celebrity-staged reading.

Richman received a Drama Critics award for his one-man show *4 Faces* which he wrote and appeared in in Los Angeles and in New York. He also wrote, produced and starred in the film vision which received a Prism Award commendation. He has also written the novel *"Hollander's Deal,"* as well as a book of short stores, *"The Rebirth of Ira Masters,"* and recently completed his autobiography *"I Saw a Molten White Light."*

David Rintels

Emmy Award-winning David Rintels began writing episodic drama in the early 1960s for *The Defenders, Slattery's People*, and later for *The F.B.I.*

In 1967 he became associate producer of *The Invaders* during their second season. Throughout the 1970s, 1980s and 1990s he focused more on writing long-form television as well as producing many of his projects.

His television work as a writer/producer includes: *The Member of the Wedding, Andersonville, World War II: When Lions Roared, The Last Best Year* (Emmy), *Day One, Gideon's Trumpet*, and *Washington: Behind Closed Doors*.

As a writer: *Nuremberg, Sakharov, Fear on Trial* (Emmy), and *Clarence Darrow* (Emmy). As Executive Producer/Producer: *My Antonia, The Execution of Raymond Graham, Choices of the Heart, All the Way Home*, and *The Oldest Living Graduate*.

Alfred Ryder

Veteran actor Alfred Ryder was an established New York stage actor long before he began to work in films and television. He began his theatrical career at the age of eight on Broadway and eventually he became an accomplished stage director. Ryder made his film debut in *Winged Victory* (1943).

His film work includes *Tracks, Escape to Witch Mountain, The Legend of Hillbilly John, The Stone Killer, True Grit, Hotel, Invitation to a Gunfighter, Hamlet, The Raiders, The Story on Page One, T-Men*, and *Golden Slippers*.

His many network television credits include: *Bogie, Buck Rodgers in the 25th Century, Quincy M.E., Charlie's Angels, The Streets of San Francisco, Ellery Queen, Switch, Swiss Family Robinson, The Six Million Dollar Man, Hec Ramsey, Kojak, The F.B.I., Barnaby Jones, Mannix, Search, The Bold Ones, McCloud, Bonanza, Mission Impossible, The Name of the Game, Medical Center, Hawaii Five-O, D.A.: Murder One, Land of the Giants, Ironside, Felony*

Squad, The Danny Thomas Hour, Judd for the Defense, It Takes a Thief, The Man from Uncle, The Rat Patrol, The Wild Wild West, Voyage to the Bottom of the Sea, Laredo, The Virginian, Star Trek, Ben Casey, Gunsmoke, The Long Hot Summer, The Alfred Hitchcock Hour, The Defenders, The Rogues, The Eleventh Hour, Combat, Wagon Train, The Outer Limits, Route 66, The Greatest Show on Earth, Naked City, Bus Stop, Dr. Kildare, 87th Precinct, The Untouchables, Outlaws, The Aquanauts, Five Fingers, The DuPont Show of the Month, Shirley Temple's Storybook, Robert Montgomery Presents, The Alcoa Hour, Studio One, Philco Television Playhouse, Goodyear Television Playhouse, Starlight Theatre, and *Danger.*

Kent Smith

Kent Smith began his career on the stage and by the early 1940s was appearing in feature films. With the advent of television in the 1950s, Smith frequently appeared on shows such as *The Philco Television Playhouse, Studio One, Hallmark Hall of Fame, Robert Montgomery Presents,* and *Lux Video Theater.* His productive career continued well into the 1970s.

Feature films include: *Billy Jack Goes to Washington, Big Mo, Lost Horizon, Pete 'n' Tillie, The Games, Death of a Gunfighter, Assignment to Kill, Kona Coast, The Money Jungle, Games, A Covenant with Death, The Trouble with Angels, The Young Lovers, Youngblood Hawke, A Distant Trumpet, The Balcony, Susan Slade, Strangers When We Meet, This Earth Is Mine, The Mugger, Party Girl, The Badlanders, Imitation General, Sayonara, Comanche, Paula, This Side of the Law, The Damned Don't Cry, My Foolish Heart, The Fountainhead, The Voice of the Turtle, Magic Town, Nora Prentiss, The Spiral Staircase, The Curse of the Cat People, Three Russian Girls, This Land Is Mine, Forever and a Day, Hitler's Children, Three Cadets, Cat People,* and *The Garden Murder Case.*

His television work includes: *Wonder Woman, Gibbsville, Once an Eagle, Barnaby Jones, The Disappearance of Flight 412, The Cat Creature, The Streets of San Francisco, The Affair, Night Gallery, The Judge and Jake Wyler, Owen Marshall: Counselor at*

Law, The Delphi Bureau, Probe, The Night Stalker, Another Part of the Forest, The Last Child, The Governor and J.J., The F.B.I., How Awful about Allan, The Wild Wild West, Daniel Boone, Mission Impossible, Felony Squad, The Man from U.N.C.L.E., Peyton Place (as Dr. Robert Morton), *I Spy, A Man Called Shenandoah, The Alfred Hitchcock Hour, The Great Adventure, The Eleventh Hour, Rawhide, The Outer Limits, Arrest and Trial, The Untouchables, Going My Way, The Wide Country, Perry Mason, Have Gun-Will Travel, Cain's Hundred, 77 Sunset Strip, Checkmate, Bronco, Adventures in Paradise, The Defenders, Lawman, Wagon Train, Dan Raven, Michael Shayne, The Millionaire, Naked City,* and *General Electric Theater.*

Julie Sommars

Born and raised in the Midwest, Julie Sommars first appeared in *The Loretta Young Show* (1960). She portrayed assistant district attorney Julie Marsh in the TV series *Matlock* (from 1987–1994) and co-starred as Jennifer Jo Drinkwater in *The Governor & J.J.* (1969–1970).

Her many television credits include: *Diagnosis Murder, Perry Mason: The Case of the Glass Coffin, Rituals, Emergency Room, Cave-in!, The Devlin Connection, Magnum P.I., Insight, Fantasy Island, Beyond Westworld, Barnaby Jones, Sex and the Single Parent, Centennial, McMillan & Wife, Jigsaw John, Bronk, Ellery Queen, Three for the Road, The Family Holvak, Switch, McCloud, The Rockford Files, Harry O, Sin American Style, Thriller, Owen Marshall: Counselor at Law, The Harness, Five Desperate Women, Love American Style, Lancer, The F.B.I., The Virginian, The Name of the Game, Judd for the Defense, Felony Squad, Get Smart, He and She, The Man from Uncle, The Fugitive, Bob Hope Presents the Chrysler Theater, Run Buddy Run, Gunsmoke, Death Valley Days, Ben Casey, Mr. Novak, Perry Mason, Flipper, Slattery's People, Bonanza, The Great Adventure, The Tall Men,* and *Shirley Temple's Story Book.*

Her films include: *Herbie Goes to Monte Carlo, The Pad and How to Use It, The Great Sioux Massacre,* and *The Fun Lovers.*

Susan Strasberg

Susan Strasberg, the daughter of famed acting teacher Lee Strasberg and stage actress Paula Strasberg, was a gifted actress in her own right who achieved success on the New York stage and subsequently in films and television.

She made her Broadway debut in the title role of *The Diary of Anne Frank*, and her television debut at age 15 on *The Goodyear Television Playhouse*.

Her film work includes: *Schweitzer, Prime Suspect, The Runnin' Kind, The Delta Force, Sweet 16, The Returning, In Praise of Older Women, The Manitou, Rollercoaster, Sammy Someday, The Stranger, The Legend of Hillbilly John, The Other Side of the Wind, The Brotherhood, The Trip, Chubasco, Taste of Fear, Kapo, Stage Struck, Picnic,* and *The Cobweb*.

Her television appearances include: *Cagney & Lacey, Murder She Wrote, Remington Steele, Tales from the Darkside, Tales of the Unexpected, Mike Hammer, The Love Boat, Beggarman Thief, The Immigrants, SST: Death Flight, The Rockford Files, Medical Center, Harry O, Bronk, Medical Story, Kate McShane, Ellery Queen, Petrocelli, McMillan & Wife, The Streets of San Francisco, Owen Marshall: Counselor at Law, Toma, Night Gallery, Mannix, Assignment Vienna, McCloud, Dr. Simon Locke, The Young Lawyers, Alias Smith and Jones, The Virginian, Marcus Welby M.D., The Name of the Game, Lancer, The F.B.I., Bonanza, The Big Valley, The Legend of Jesse James, Run for Your Life, Burke's Law, The Rogues, Breaking Point, Bob Hope Presents the Chrysler Theater, Dr. Kildare, Destiny West!, Westinghouse Desilu Playhouse,* and *Omnibus*.

Roy Thinnes

Roy Thinnes was born and raised in Chicago. He made his professional debut in the unsold pilot: *Chicago 212* which starred Frank Lovejoy. In the early 1960s, Thinnes began to appear in network TV series such as *The Untouchables, The Eleventh Hour,* and *Gunsmoke*. In 1963 he landed the role of Dr. Phil Brewer on

General Hospital. Two years later, Thinnes was cast as Ben Quick in *The Long Hot Summer* opposite Edmund O'Brien and Nancy Malone. After the show's cancellation in 1966, he was signed by Quinn Martin to star in *The Invaders* which aired for two seasons.

Among his post-Invaders TV series roles are Dr. James Whitman in *The Psychiatrist*, Capt. Dana Holmes in *From Here to Eternity*, Nick Hogan in *Falcon Crest*, and the dual role of Roger Collins/Rev. Trask in the nighttime revival of *Dark Shadows.*

His additional television appearances include *Law and Order: Special Victims Unit, Oz, Law and Order: Criminal Intent, The X Files, The Sopranos, D.C., Law and Order, Players, Touched by an Angel, Poltergeist: The Legacy, Terminal, Walker, Texas Ranger, Stormy Weathers, Lady Against the Odds, P.S. I Luv U, F.B.I.: The Untold Stories, An Inconvenient Woman, Murder She Wrote, War of the Worlds, Blue Bayou, Dark Holiday, Highway to Heaven, One Life to Live (as Alex Coronol), The Love Boat, Hotel, Sizzle, Scruples, Freedom, Return of the Mod Squad, Stone, Battlestar Galactica, Code Name: Diamond Head, Secrets, Death Race, Satan's School for Girls, The Norliss Tapes, The Horror at 37,000 Feet, The Manhunter, Black Noon, The Other Man, The Fugitive, Twelve O'Clock High, The F.B.I., The Reporter,* and *Peter Gunn. Film work includes Leadcatcher, Broken English, Undone, Spectropia, The Eyes of Van Gogh, A Beautiful Mind. The Hindenburg, Airport 1975, Charley One-Eye,* and *Journey to the Far Side of the Sun.*

Thinnes is also an accomplished artist with gallery showings in Texas, California and Tennessee.

Jack Warden

A former boxer and veteran of the U.S. Navy, U.S. Army as well as the Merchant Marines, Jack Warden first became interested in the acting profession while serving in World War II. After the war he studied under the G.I. Bill and later joined the Dallas Alley Theatre where he performed in repertory.

He made his Broadway debut in *Golden Boy* (1952) and his film debut (a year earlier) in *You're in the Navy Now*. His work in films and network television spanned almost five decades. His TV series include *The Asphalt Jungle* (1961), *The Wackiest Ship in the Army* (1964–1965), *N.Y.P.D.* (1967–1969), *Jigsaw John* (1976), and *Crazy Like a Fox* (1984–1986).

Film work includes: *The Replacements, A Dog of Flanders, Bulworth, Chairman of the Board, The Volunteers, Ed, Mighty Aphrodite, While You Were Sleeping, Bullets Over Broadway, Guilty as Sin, Toys, Night and the City, Problem Child 2, Problem Child, Everybody Wins, The Presidio, Aviator, Crackers, The Verdict, So Fine, Chu Chu and the Philly Flash, Carbon Copy, Used Cars, Being There, And Justice for All, Beyond the Poseidon Adventure, Dreamer, The Champ, Death on the Nile, Heaven Can Wait, The White Buffalo, All the President's Men, Shampoo, Billy Two Hats, Who Is Harry Kellerman and Why Is He Saying Terrible Things about Me?, Summertree, Bye Bye Braverman, Donovan's Reef, Escape from Zahrain, Wake Me When It's Over, The Sound and the Fury, Run Silent Run Deep, Darby's Rangers, 12 Angry Men, The Bachelor Party, Edge of the City,* and *From Here to Eternity.*

Television appearances include: *The Norm Show, Ink, Knight & Dave, Policy Story: The Watch Commander, The Three Kings, Three Wishes for Jamie, Robert Kennedy and His Times, Helen Keller: The Miracle Continues, A Private Battle, Topper, The Bad News Bears, Raid on Entebbe, The Godchild, Man on a String, Brian's Song, A Memory of Two Mondays, The Fugitive, Wagon Train, The Virginian, Dr. Kildare, Disneyland, Slattery's People, Bob Hope Presents the Chrysler Theater, Bewitched, Kraft Suspense Theatre, The Great Adventure, Breaking Point, Route 66, 77 Sunset Strip, Naked City, Ben Casey, Going My Way, Alcoa Premiere, Target: The Corruptors, Tales of Wells Fargo, Bus Stop, Checkmate, The Untouchables, Outlaws, Stagecoach West, The Twilight Zone, Westinghouse Desilu Playhouse, Five Fingers, Bonanza, Playhouse 90, Suspicion, The United States Steel Hour, Hallmark Hall of Fame, Climax, The Philco Television Playhouse, Producers' Showcase, Kraft Television Theatre, Studio One, Inner Sanctum, Man Against Crime, Mister Peepers,* and *Tales of Tomorrow.*

Dawn Wells

A former Miss Nevada in the 1960 Miss America Pageant, Dawn Wells studied drama in college, then decided to pursue a professional acting career. After appearing in numerous episodic TV shows in the early 1960s, Wells was cast as Mary Ann Summers in *Gilligan's Island* (1964–1967). Throughout the years she has appeared on various television series as well as performed in regional theaters across the country.

Her television credits include: *Pastor Greg, Three Sisters, Meego, Roseanne, TV's All-Time Favorites, Herman's Head, Baywatch, Growing Pains, ALF, High School USA, Matt Houston, The Harlem Globetrotters on Gilligan's Island, Fantasy Island, The Love Boat, Hagen, The Castaways on Gilligan's Island, Vegas, Rescue from Gilligan's Island, The F.B.I., Bonanza, The Wild Wild West, Burke's Law, Channing, Laramie, Ripcord, It's a Man's World, Hawaiian Eye, Surfside Six, Lawman, 87th Precinct, Tales of Wells Fargo, Everglades, The Detectives Starring Robert Taylor, 77 Sunset Strip, Wagon Train, Cheyenne, Maverick,* and *The Roaring Twenties.*

Her film credits include: *Forever for Now, Lover's Knot, Soulmates, The Princess and the Dwarf, The Town That Dreaded Sundown, Winterhawk, The New Interns,* and *Palm Springs Weekend.*

Paul Wendkos

Award-winning director Paul Wendkos amassed a diverse yet consistently excellent body of work. He directed more than 100 MOWs, miniseries and episodic dramas in a 50-year career.

Wendkos arrived in Hollywood with an independent film, *The Burglar* (starring Jayne Mansfield in her first movie role), and was signed by Columbia Pictures. A sampling of his directorial accomplishments and award-winning MOWs and miniseries include: *A Woman Called Moses, Death of Richie, Picking Up the Pieces, Farrell for the People, Right to Die, Cocaine: One Man's Seduction, Guilty Until Proven Innocent,* and *The Ordeal of Dr. Mudd.*

He also received Emmy nominations for *Brotherhood of the Bell, The Legend of Lizzie Borden, The Taking of Flight 847*, and *Blind Faith.*

Additional television movies and miniseries include: *Different, On a Wing and a Prayer, Match Made in Heaven, Nobody Lives Forever, Cry for Love, Betrayal, Secrets, Act of Violence, The Five of Me, Scorned and Swindled, Honor Thy Father, Blood Vows, The Bad Seed, The Woman I Love, The Execution, From the Dead of Night, Bloodlines, The Trial, Celebrity, 79 Park Avenue, The Great Escape II, Rage of Angels*, and *Cross of Fire.*

His theatrical films include: *Mephisto Waltz, Special Delivery, Angel Baby, Gidget*, and *Guns of the Magnificent Seven.*

James Whitmore

A veteran of the Broadway stage and feature films, James Whitmore later enjoyed the same success in television.

His film work includes *The Majestic, Here's to Life, The Relic, The Shawshank Redemption, Old Explorers, Nuts, The First Deadly Sin, Give 'em Hell Harry!, Where the Red Fern Grows, The Harrod Experiment, Chato's Land, Tora! Tora! Tora!, Guns of the Magnificent Seven, The Split, Madigan, Planet of the Apes, Nobody's Perfect, Waterhole #3, Chuka, Black Like Me, Who Was That Lady?, Face of Fire, The Deep Six, The Young Don't Cry, The Eddie Duchin Story, Crime in the Streets, The Last Frontier, Oklahoma, The McConnell Story, Battle Cry, Them, The Command, All the Brothers Were Valiant, Kiss Me Kate, The Girl Who Had Everything, Above and Beyond, Because You're Mine, Shadow in the Sky, It's a Big Country, The Next Voice You Hear, The Asphalt Jungle, Please Believe Me, The Outriders, Battleground*, and *The Undercover Man.*

Television appearances: *C.S.I., Mister Sterling, The Practice, The Ray Bradbury Theater, All My Sons, Riptide, Celebrity, The White Shadow, Rage, The Word, The Canterville Ghost, Gunsmoke, Temperatures Rising, If Tomorrow Comes, The Virginian, Then Came Bronson, The Name of the Game, My Friend Tony* (as Prof. John Woodruff), *Bonanza, The Danny Thomas Hour, Cowboy in Africa, The Big Valley, Custer, Judd for the Defense, Tarzan, 12 O'Clock High, The Monroes, Shane, T.H.E. Cast, The Loner, Run for Your Life, Burke's Law, Combat, Disneyland, Arrest and Trial, Dr. Kildare, The Twilight Zone, Ben Casey, Route 66, Going My Way, The Detectives Starring Robert Taylor, Checkmate, Alcoa Premiere, Frontier Justice, Zane Grey Theater, Playhouse 90, Wagon Train, Panic!, Climax, Kraft Television Theater,* and *Schlitz Playhouse of Stars.*

Glenn Wilder

Glenn Wilder has enjoyed a lengthy career as a stuntman, stunt coordinator, actor, and second unit director that has spanned five decades and taken him all over the world.

He began his career in 1960, in the feature film *High-Time* that starred Bing Crosby, doubling actor/singer Fabian and eventually worked as a second unit director on such films as *Terminator 2: Judgement Day, True Lies, Presidio, March or Die* and the acclaimed miniseries *Shogun.* He most recently worked on the films *Wanderlust* starring Jennifer Aniston, as well as *Journey 2: The Mysterious Island,* starring Michael Caine and Dwayne Johnson.

William Windom

William Windom made his debut with the American Repertory Theatre (1946). In the 1950s, in addition to his continued work in the theater, Windom appeared on television in *Masterpiece Playhouse, Omnibus, Robert Montgomery Presents,* and *Hallmark Hall of Fame.*

He made his film debut in *To Kill a Mockingbird* (1962). In series TV he co-starred as Congressman Glenn Morley opposite Inger Stevens in *The Farmer's Daughter* (1963–1966), and won critical acclaim for his portrayal of cartoonist John Monroe in the James Thurber-inspired *My World and Welcome to It*

(1969–1970). He was also seen as Dr. Seth Hazlitt on *Murder, She Wrote* (1985–1996).

His film work includes: *Just, Yesterday's Dreams, True Crime, Sommersby, Street Justice, She's Having a Baby, Committed, Funland, Welcome Home, Grandview USA, Echoes of a Summer, The Man, The Mephisto Waltz, Escape from Planet of the Apes, Fool's Parade, Brewster McCloud, The Gypsy Moths, The Detective, The Angry Breed, Hour of the Gun, The Americanization of Emily, One Man's Way, For Love or Money,* and *Cattle King.*

His many TV appearances include: *Star Trek: New Voyages, JAG, The District, Providence, Ally McBeal, Judging Amy, Boy Meets Girl, Burke's Law, Murphy Brown, L.A. Law, The Fanelli Boys, Parenthood, Newhart, Magnum P.I., Knight Rider, Airwolf, Hardcastle and McCormack, Hotel, Highway To Heaven, Hunter, The Yellow Rose, Simon & Simon, St. Elsewhere, Automan, The Facts of Life, Matt Houston, Mama's Family, The A-Team, The Greatest American Hero, The Love Boat, Trapper John M.D., Hart to Hart, Fantasy Island, Barney Miller, Dallas, W.E.B., Kojak, Family, Quincy M.E., Police Woman, Seventh Avenue, McMillan & Wife, The Tony Randall Show, Once an Eagle, Gibbsville, The Bionic Woman, The Streets of San Francisco, Petrocelli, Mannix, S.W.A.T., Lucas Tanner, Hawkins, Mission Impossible, The F.B.I., Love American Style, The Rookies, Gunsmoke, Banacek, Ironside, Marcus Welby M.D., Cannon, The Virginian, That Girl, The Name of the Game, The House on Greenapple Road, U.M.C., Lancer, The Mod Squad, Bonanza, Prescription: Murder, Judd for the Defense, Gentle Ben, Star Trek, The Fugitive, Run for Your Life, 12 O'Clock High, 77 Sunset Strip, Empire, The Twilight Zone, Combat, Stoney Burke, Thriller, The Donna Reed Show, Bus Stop, Surfside Six, Cheyenne, Checkmate, Ben Casey, The New Breed,* and *The Detectives Starring Robert Taylor.*

Dana Wynter

Dana Wynter has led an interesting life as an actress, author, journalist, and activist. She began her life in Berlin and later spent her formative years in Scotland and England. After a year of medical study at Rhodes University in South Africa, she returned to England and began to work in the English theater. In the early 1950s she went to New York and subsequently appeared in live television and on Broadway. She signed a seven-year contract with 20th Century Fox in 1955. She starred in a number of feature films on into the early 1960s, then began to guest in numerous network TV series.

In the mid-1960s, Wynter took up journalism with her own by-line in *The Guardian* (the oldest and most prestigious English newspaper). She also wrote articles for *National Review, Country Living, Image, The Irish Times* and others. In recent years her book *Other People, Other Places* (essays about her life and memories on four continents) was published by Caladrius Press, Dublin.

Her film work includes *Santee, Airport, The List of Adrian Messenger, On the Double, Sink the Bismarck, Shake Hands with the Devil, In Love and War, Fraulein, Something of Value, Invasion of the Body Snatchers, D-Day—Sixth of June,* and *View from Pompey's Head.*

Her many television appearances include *Dana Wynter in Ireland* (PBS), *The Royal Romance of Charles and Diana, Backstairs at the White House, Magnum P.I., Hart to Hart, The Love Boat, Hawaii Five-O, Fantasy Island, City of Angels, Ellery Queen, Medical Center, Cannon, Ironside, Owen Marshall-Counselor at Law, Marcus Welby M.D., Gunsmoke, Love American Style, The Name of the Game, The Wild Wild West, The Man Who Never Was* (as Eva Wainwright), *The F.B.I., Twelve O'Clock High, The Rogues, The Alfred Hitchcock Hour, Wagon Train, The Virginian, The Dick Powell Theater, Playhouse 90, Twentieth Century Fox Hour, Studio One, U.S. Steel Hour,* and *Suspicion.*

ENDNOTES

1. Larry Cohen, telephone interview—May 2009, California

2. Alan Armer, telephone interview—May 2009, California

3. Ralph Senensky, telephone interview—June 2009, California

4. Don Eitner, telephone interview—June 2009, California

5. Marshall Schlom, telephone interview—May 2009, California

6. Roy Thinnes, from an interview with Joel Blumberg on *Silver Screen Audio*—April 2008, New York

7. David Rintels, telephone interview—May 2009, California

8. Robert Day, telephone interview—May 2009, Washington

9. Howard Alston, telephone interview—May 2009, California

10. William Hale, telephone interview—May 2009, Virginia

11. Stephen Bowie, from his essay: *The Invaders: Behind the Scenes*—classictvhistory.com

12. Paul Wurtzel, telephone interview—June 2009, California

13. Tom Lowell, telephone interview—July 2009, California

14. Carl Barth, telephone interview—June 2009, California

15. John Elizalde, telephone interview—June 2009, California

16. Duane Tatro, telephone interview—July 2009, California

17. Roy Thinnes, telephone interview—June 2009, New York

Also by **James Rosin**

ADVENTURES IN RPARADISE: The Television Series

NAKED CITY: The Television Series

PEYTON PLACE: The Television Series

PHILADELPHIA, CITY OF MUSIC

PHILLY HOOPS: The SPHAS and Warriors

QUINCY M.E.: The Television Series

ROCK, RHYTHM AND BLUES

ROUTE 66: The Television Series

THE STREETS OF SAN FRANCISCO:
A Quinn Martin TV Series

WAGON TRAIN: The Television Series

ABOUT THE AUTHOR

BORN AND RAISED in Philadelphia, James Rosin graduated from Temple University's School of Communications with a degree in broadcasting. In New York, he studied acting with Bobby Lewis and appeared in plays off-off Broadway and on the ABC soap opera, *Edge of Night*. In Los Angeles, Rosin played featured and costarring roles in such TV series as *Mickey Spillane's Mike Hammer, T.J. Hooker, Quincy M.E., The Powers of Matthew Star, Cannon, Mannix, Banacek, Adam-12, Love, American Style,* and two miniseries, *Loose Change* and *Once an Eagle.* His film credits include *Up Close and Personal, Sleepers* and *The Adventures of Buckaroo Banzai.* He also wrote stories and teleplays for *Quincy M.E.* (NBC), *Capitol* (CBS), and *Loving Friends and Perfect Couples* (Showtime). His full-length play, *Michael in Beverly Hills,* premiered at American Theater Arts in Los Angeles and was later presented off-off Broadway, at the American Musical Dramatic Academy's Studio One Theater.

In recent years, Rosin has written and produced two one-hour sports documentaries which have aired on public television: *Philly Hoops: The SPHAS and Warriors* (about the first two professional basketball teams in the City of Philadelphia), and *The Philadelphia Athletics 1901–1954* (about the former American

League franchise), both recently released by Alpha Video. His first book, *Philly Hoops: The SPHAS and Warriors* was published in 2003, followed by *Rock, Rhythm and Blues* (2004), *Philadelphia: City of Music* (2006), *Route 66: The Television Series* (2007, revised 2011), *Naked City: The Television Series* (2008), *Wagon Train: The Television Series* (2008, revised 2011), *Adventures in Paradise: The Television Series* (2009), *Quincy M.E.: The Television Series* (2009), *The Invaders: A Quinn Martin TV Series* and *Peyton Place: The Television Series* (both in 2010), and *The Streets of San Francisco: A Quinn Martin TV Series* (2011).

He has also been a contributing writer to *Classic Images* and *Films of the Golden Age Magazine.*

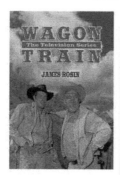
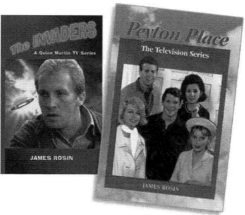

A LOOK BACK at our memorable classic television series featuring commentary from show's lead actors, guest stars, episode summaries, photos, and biographies.

Here's what readers and reviewers are saying about author JAMES ROSIN's TV books...

> *"His access to many of the original cast and crew gives this offering a solid credibility."*

> *"...series fans will enjoy the history, photos and storytelling"*

> *"Filled with interesting details that will please most enthusiasts of the series."*

Order your copies today at: www.**classictvseriesbooks**.com

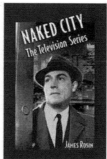

Printed in Great Britain
by Amazon

42930622R00118